G. Z. Leligdowicz
2 Lochmore
Achfary
By Lairg
Sutherland IV27 4NZ
01971 500 238

Happy 50th Gary —

Best wishes from
all at Serse

Jamie Farquhar

THE GHILLIE
A CURE FOR STRESS

SECURE WITH JIM LAST
A salmon, Lower Scone Beat, The Tay

THE GHILLIE
A CURE FOR STRESS

Dr. James M. Dyce

Illustrations by Iain M. Dyce

James M Dyce

INTRODUCTION
by
Mick Lunn
Head Keeper, (Third generation), The
Houghton Club,

Stress Publications

First published 1987
Stress Publications
47 Water Street, Lavenham, Suffolk CO10 9RN

British Library Cataloguing in Publication Data
Dyce, James M.
  The ghillie, a cure for stress.
  1. Fishing
  I. Title
  799.1′2′0924   SH439

ISBN 0-9508277-4-6

Printed in Great Britain by
The Lavenham Press
Water Street, Lavenham, Suffolk CO10 9RN

THANK YOU to my encouragers and advisers:

Sir Terence G. Ward, Past President, The International Association of Oral and Maxillo Facial Surgeons *who first proposed that I write this book*

Professor M. H. M. Harrison, past president, British Orthopaedic Research Society, Hunterian Professor, Royal College of Surgeons, England

Brig. Sir Geoffrey Hardy-Roberts, K.C.V.O.; C.B.; C.V.O.; J.P.

T. A. F. Norcliffe, B.D.S. (Hons), Harley Street, London

Edward Goulding, M.A. (Oxon)

Jean Goodman, Journalist and Biographer, author of the forthcoming biography of Sir Alfred Munnings

Leonard Brown, Production Director, A. & C. Black (Publishers) Ltd

John Russell, Managing Director, The ORVIS Co., Inc., Nether Wallop Mill, Stockbridge, Hampshire

Fred H. E. Buller, Chubbs Ltd., Little Chalfont, Bucks

P. Cockburn-Mercer, House of Hardy, Pall Mall, London

Peter Naylor, Trout and Salmon Magazine, Peterborough

And my wife

CONTENTS

INTRODUCTION
MICK LUNN

*Head Keeper, (Third generation), The
Houghton Club, The River Test,
Stockbridge, Hampshire*

I have been lucky to be on both sides of the
fence, a keeper producing fishing and all
that goes with it on the one hand and enjoying
my annual busman's holidays in places like
Scotland, Iceland and Norway, being the pri-
vileged fisherman, so I understand well the
behaviour of the ghillie. I must confess that
wherever I have been those I have met have
most of the qualities I am about to describe.

I have also been extremely fortunate in my
life to have a job which in a sense is my hobby.
All true keepers/ghillies must feel the same – it
is a way of life.

I've always felt that a first class ghillie should
be endowed with many attributes. He should be
a good companion to his angler and an encoura-
ger, especially for the not so good fisher. He
must know his river, the favourite lies of the
fish and must be acquainted with all the species
of bugs and flies which emerge from the river
and their life cycle and those that frequent the
waterside and the times of the year one would
expect to find them. He would be familiar with
the water weeds and the wild flowers and trees
which grow on the banks. The birds and
animals are also of great interest.

He needs to be a man of considerable patience
who through the years especially on trout
rivers, has developed the eye for spotting a good

fish rise and deciding from this its size and whether a trout or grayling. His choice of the artificial fly will be needed by the angler and the speed with which he attaches it to the cast will be appreciated especially when the light is failing. Besides tying knots he will be sorely tried at untying knots and tangles by an ill-timed cast or the much maligned wind. He will take care of all the paraphernalia a fisherman carries and produce the bits and pieces as required, dry fly, fly dressing, scissors or net and of course be the pack mule and carry the catch.

He must not be like a dog at heel with the gentleman fishing and must not say too little or be a chatter-box either and refrain from giving a running commentary on every cast the fisherman makes. Not too many cracks like: "You should have been here yesterday." or "You would be better at home or in the Hotel, there isn't a fish in the river." After all the angler has probably paid quite a sum for the privilege and it is the highlight of his year.

A ghillie must never be a pessimist, he *must* be an optimist, making a good case for his river with the 'white lie' always being available. After all fishing has so many good things to be said for it. It takes you to beautiful places and works a kind of therapy on those that take part, coming from their offices, operating theatres or whatever, looking rather maggoty and pale; a rod in the hand by the water's edge and the anticipation of a few fishing days ahead has the knack of making all one's cares disappear and a transformation in looks, spirit and peace of mind can be seen. I've seen a senior consulting surgeon, exhausted by his intensive work, look ten years younger after a few hours by the river.

There is little doubt that longevity and fishing go together, it is quite extraordinary the age anglers attain. There is a maxim which says: "Hours spent fishing are not included in your normal span of life."

So, anglers, do not lose sight of the fact that there is more to fishing than catching fish and a ghillie is a pleasant and helpful companion who spends his time with nature and if he has made your visit to his river a memorable one then his praises will be sung by you wherever you go.

Mick Lunn,

Stockbridge,
July 1987

Further thoughts on why ghillies/keepers have an in-built skill in dealing with stress are revealed in talks with Mick, in the chapter: *Guardians of a Heritage.*

THE TOAST

FISHING is not about the hundred best artificial flies and how to land them on the water like a butterfly with sore feet, nor is it about floating or sinking lines, nor is it about rods of various lengths and weights, although a lot of people think it is.

Fishing is about a way of life which takes us into a dimension beyond our special interests and there are times in life when we need this. Every one of us is special, with a unique contribution to make to world affairs. Re-evaluating the pressures of life and the mysteries of stress is necessary treatment for the success seeker.

The ghillie is a man who can give comradeship for this adventure. And he is usually understanding of our weary bones and inefficiency in his department. He is as committed to the hills, the lochans, the streams, as most of us are to our Balance Sheet. He opens up one more window on the universe.

A quick day out tends to have a target – "a basket" – but that is a questionable approach to fishing. We say we haven't time, then we are being swept along by the tide. Fishing is about taking time to understand what is needed to turn the tide. There are worlds beyond the world we see. Life-science is a must if we are to avoid becoming irrelevant in a world of specialists who do not have the wisdom to foresee the future with its unpredictable possibilities.

Trout have many lessons to teach us as they shadow around at the bottom of a stream awaiting the arrival of food. They have a life fully part of all that is going on in nature – the light, the shade, the heat, the cold, the rise and fall of the water level, rushing tumbling spate water, peaceful places under trees or among the willows; in dangerous shallows or in deep pools well away from the stabbing heron and other predators.

The ghillie, who spends his life with these phenomena readily responds if we pay attention to him first, and that is where fishing begins. His life is lived in terms of the seasons and the years, in contrast to the successful among us who are tuned to work against the clock.

Three weeks with a ghillie brings us back to fundamentals. Of course, that is what we think we have been doing until the day we left for 'the fishing'. We have been reacting to events. The ghillie's mind stands back from events. The things he says, the way he thinks, the things we see around us, the time we get to think, to uncoil, to relax, to stop thinking, to be refreshed, to find fresh inspiration for the future, produce the complementary requirement for living today.

In his own special way, probably without saying a word to you, the ghillie will help you understand more about today's missing elements.

1
Sage and Dominie

PENETRATING HIS COUNTRY

MY APPRENTICESHIP BEGINS WITH
DONALD CAMPBELL OF SUTHERLAND

MUST YOU HAVE IMMEDIATE
RESULTS?

THERE'S A LOT OF LONG SCOTS "OH"s,
BUT THAT'S MY CAMPBELL

NOW WE MOVE ON TO CHARACTER
BUILDING

PENETRATING HIS COUNTRY

THIS story has a happy ending. By the time I had served my apprenticeship with Donald and Robbie in Sutherland I had fished thirty-two different lochs and caught thirty-six trout.

Fourteen years in my profession had passed before I tried fishing. The trout in the glass case on the wall of the study are reminders that fishing does something very special. Much of this specialness was supplied by highland ghillies, those good companions who sort out a philosophy of life.

Actually, after many fishing trips, I am still an apprentice and even more dependent on the companionship of a ghillie. So here are recorded backward reflections about those countrymen who have a cure for stress.

With the ups and downs of busy practice, becoming senior partner and becoming part of the world lecture circuit, I was not too excited about leaving Harley Street on Friday evening. I felt I was running away in the midst of a host of uncompleted jobs. Things would be even busier as the summer moved on, so it would pay to be jolly fit for it.

Preparations for days and weeks had been going on for this expedition, acquiring bottles for collecting and preserving flies, woollen garments galore, fishing rods (borrowed), camera equipment (parts of a dark room). It was all packed in six pieces of baggage.

The 7.20 p.m. Inverness train had good sleepers. We stopped only at Crewe, then Perth, then many little stations to Inverness. Some of these stops only occur when passengers tell the guard they want to get off; 7.0 a.m. at Killie-crankie. What a sight! It was beautiful. The sun shone on the snow-capped mountains all round. The river Garry runs alongside the track for nearly a mile. It was May and the railway banks had huge clumps of primroses. The trees and fields were very pale green, and were soon replaced by the wild moorland of the Grampian mountains, as I tucked into Scots porridge, nice gritty stuff. I didn't want to miss a thing, including the bacon and eggs.

After Speyside and the rising streams which will become the river Findhorn, came the long hill down past Culloden Muir, a place where the history of Scotland changed course, then the fine views of the Moray Firth to Inverness. There I picked up my two other rods and hovered in Grant's tartan shop to look over the alternative Dyce family crests and so to the friendly John O'Groats train at 10.40 a.m. It appeared to stop for a chat everywhere. At Dingwall the engine left altogether to move a truck or two. Lunch on the train was good: Soup, Venison, Cabinet pudding as light as a sponge with fruit inside – a second helping of that. At Lairg, about 1.30 p.m. I got off with two or three other fishermen to await the departure of 'The Mails' bus service to the 'outpost of Empire' at Kinlochbervie. This unique bus service is the only communication with the world from these parts. A very single track fifty mile road to the West coast of Sutherland. The back section of The Mails had no seats and was filled with everything imaginable, while the roof too took its share.

Accepting that the bus driver was 'the regu-lar' relieved my terror. A fellow fishing resident later described his experience thus: "We came hurtling along the single track at a reckless pace. Every hundred yards there was a big bump or a blind corner or a drop of several hundred feet down to some loch side. The driver looks like Tam O'Shanter. He stops every few miles and nothing happens at all for five or ten minutes. They may have had a meal or a drink, then on again at breakneck speed."

He continued some days later: "Today we boarded the bus. Thought it must be full of people. It looked like it through the wind and squall of rain. Inside however were large bags of mail, huge boxes of bread and baggage and some small heifers and bicycles. There were some fishermen going to join a drifter at Kinlochbervie. The fisher lads were all dressed up in the finest blue suits, fit for Piccadilly. I was wet through even to the seat of my pants, having been fishing in the howling rain and wind all day. The little bus was then so full I could barely stand up beside the driver."

As they hurtled along the switchback, my fishing friend was thrown in the air and bumped his head on the roof. He had the greatest difficulty maintaining his feet, with people rolling about amid the assorted baggage including radio batteries which had been to the local garage for recharging. Meanwhile his wife did get a seat next to a wifie with a baby with the hiccoughs. The baby's milk bottle kept leaking, so an exciting time was had by all.

The very impressive countryside is one mass of mountains, lochs, moors, peat bogs, sea lochs and here and there a few crofts. The colours are spirit-stirring. The sea changes colour all the time. Some ways you look at it, it is silvery. The next way it is green and soon the distant parts will have a wonderful deep hue. At Kinlochbervie there is a fine small harbour with fishing boats which go out to sea every day except Sunday. Their catch is sent down by road and off to the South. Far out to sea can be seen a mountain in the Outer Hebrides, about forty miles away.

Next day, Sunday, no fishing, so climbing over the hills was just the thing. I saw a black rabbit and a black lamb, so there should be some luck. Later, the fishing proprietor took me off to meet some ghillies at their cottages.

MY APPRENTICESHIP
BEGINS WITH DONALD
CAMPBELL OF
SUTHERLAND

WE CLIMBED over wild country for more than two miles till we reached a fine looking loch. It was very narrow at one place and about one mile long. I was having my first outing with the Head Keeper of the Forest, one Donald Campbell. We had already driven five miles from the lodge before setting out on foot.

It really was a fine sight. As a weakly town-man it was a help to sit and be rowed about. Campbell busied himself putting the cast on my line. Three flies on these lochan casts. The end fly, or tail, was a Grouse and Claret. It had wings of grouse feathers and a claret coloured tummy with silver stripes. The next fly, the bottom dropper was a Grouse and Green. It had wings of grouse feathers and a green body with silver stripes. The top fly on the top dropper, was a Pennel worm, jet black, a colourful tail and a silver striped stomach.

This loch is one of at least twenty on which the Hotel has 'the fishing'. Immediately to the East and also to the North are two mountains, nearly 3,000 feet high. It was quite a warm day. Sometimes it was really hot until at times the wind blew a bit and brought a nip to the air.

Campbell made me sit at the stern of the boat, so I was free to learn to cast in a wide arc. He knew I was an apprentice. Loch fishing is a good place for the beginner to start – no trees. The system of loch fishing is usually 'drifting'.

The boat moves gently before the wind and approaches fresh water all the time, so the mess the beginner makes of the first ten casts will not affect the fresh water ahead. And there might be a 'self-hooking' fish right there in line of that perfect cast. So hopes remain high, and Campbell captained the boat. There is more to that than may be imagined, holding it by skill, so that I am always in the best position.

To cut a long story short, I did not catch anything.

Reason – always necessary for a fisherman:

1. The trout were not rising to the surface to feed. I only saw three flies on the water.
2. The water was a bit too cold at the surface, as there was still some snow to come down off the mountains.
3. If the fish are not rising you cannot catch them.
4. The wind should stay in one quarter all day and not blow sometimes from one direction and half an hour later from another. Moving in one direction only, the food which fish eat tends to drift into the bays at the far end of the lochans. More concentration, more fish.
5. There were too many hours when there was no ripple on the water at all. Just like a mirror glass it was.
6. We saw some trout rise at the place where the burn runs out of the loch. They were 'cruising' trout, swimming along on the surface not looking for food (says Campbell).
7. At the top end of the loch where a stream enters, I sat in the boat in the rapid water among big boulders and cast at the current just as it runs into the open loch. Once, a trout did jump at my fly. He missed it, silly fish. He probably had no intentions.

So, there's enough excuses.

In my ignorance in handling a trout rod, one cast ended with the fly tucked into Campbell's bonnet.

All a bit different from town life. I needed a little spot of brandy when I got back to base, then a good meal and a long sleep.

All very exhilarating.

I had been really cared for all day.

Campbell's bonnet

MUST YOU HAVE
IMMEDIATE RESULTS?

MIST galore coming in off the sea this Tuesday morning, the sun overhead trying to break through. Reading the weather is one of the ghillie's skills. An unpromising start to days on the hill can be magically different by the afternoon.

However, out we went and drove four miles, then walked for half an hour over the hills. This loch is on a headland jutting out to sea and a few hundred feet above sea-level. There was quite a rough surface on the water. The mist was down so you couldn't see the other side of the loch 200 yards away. The wind was blowing and by lunch time I was regretting that fishing was as cold as mountaineering.

At a quarter to one we decided to stop. I had a whole flask of coffee, though I wasn't feeling hungry. Then I put on all the sweaters I had brought and also my waterproof overtrousers to help keep the wind out.

I kept casting with my rod and three flies. The mist rose just enough to see the sides clearly. There was enough wind to cause the boat to drift down easily and rapidly from one end to the other. Campbell kept her at an angle so that I could cast and recast my line with ease; it is necessary as an apprentice to have no trees or other obstructions when all your attention is given to landing that cast of flies on the water with no splash.

Here we were then approaching the end of two days' continuous fishing, without result. I was a little downhearted.

Then suddenly there was a trout on my line. I pulled up the top of my rod twice to make the hook fast, though I think he came at the fly so fast he hooked himself without aid.

Then learning the art of playing a fish began. A lot of things happen at once. One important thing seems to be the way the ghillie handles the boat. He kept it moving as he called out things for me to do. "Keep the tension on the line", meant that I had to keep the line tight. If the fish came towards me I had to wind the line in. Next moment he'd dash away. Then it was necessary to hold the rod, but not the line. It quickly ticked out from the reel. Next moment the fish came to the surface and leapt into the air. Would the panic-stricken trout, tail flying, break the fine cast holding the hook? Campbell shouted to me to drop the point of the rod. It is necessary to dip the point smartly to water level and make the whole line slack otherwise the tail might catch the tight cast and break it. Next moment Campbell calls to keep the rod point high in the air, which immediately puts tension back on the fish which is now deep underwater.

The trout whistled off again. Out went the line, singing off the reel. It stopped, the tension got slacker and I wound in some line. Meanwhile Campbell was rowing the boat away from the fish. There was less tension as the fish followed and I wound more line in to keep the rod top bent. Then he called to watch I didn't wind the line in so that the cast (9 ft long) came through the top eye of the rod. If that joining knot had gone through the top eyelet, and the fish had decided to dash off again, the knot might have become stuck and there would have been no line to let out so it would break the cast.

All this had to be played off the stern of the boat. Now Campbell called to turn the rod point toward him. This brought the fighting fish up the side of the boat, where he swished the landing net under it and missed, swore, pushed it out again and got it the second time.

Thus was landed a fine brown trout weighing just under three quarters of a pound. And there it sits – 'Made up' – beside me as I write this. Inscribed: Lochanant Saie. Kinlochbervie 10th May. 'My first trout'.

Strange to relate, it didn't take the end fly but the one nearest the rod, the top dropper ('the bob'). This fly, the Black Pennel is a favourite in these parts.

It was still rather cold and misty and we decided to go and have a shot at the next loch. It was a fifteen minutes' walk through the mist. By 4.30 p.m. I had cast my flies on every square yard and no fish were rising, so we stopped at 5.0 p.m.

By this time the mist rose and what a splendid sight there was, clear blue skies, wild mountains, more lochs and a view for thirty miles down the coast to Ross-shire.

It was a perfect evening. Very hot.

My face was red with the wind and weather and some sun. My seat was sore as I had been persuaded not to carry my Dunlopillo. I will tomorrow. My arms ached. New muscles had come into use. My right wrist was aching.

But there's nothing like success to open the mind to the whole horizon. Donald had introduced me to the moorlands and the lochs and there was a uniformity between these features and the man with whom I spent two days.

THERE'S A LOT OF LONG SCOTS "OH"s, BUT THAT'S MY CAMPBELL

IT WAS a late start, as we had to wait on the local joiner finishing the oars. I understand they had been on order for some two years. At first we could not find Cameron the joiner, and as it was only 10.00 a.m. it was suggested that he might not be up yet. Oh, there's no great hurry up here.

The boat had not been out on the loch this season and both Campbell the Head Keeper and the Proprietor were very optimistic about the results awaiting us. Quite a nice day, this third fishing day.

Anyway, we got down to the Riconich river where the main road crosses it. This is about 5 miles from the Hotel. The road, by the way, is not even a third class one. We walked steadily by burn, up hill, over moors, through bogs 'till 12.23 p.m. In just over one hour and thirty-five minutes we had arrived at our loch.

It was a good day for fishing. Now, what is a good day for fishing? Nobody knows, if you ask me now.

Anyway, it was cold, but not nearly as cold as yesterday. The water was warmer. There were patches of blue sky, blinks of sun, a nice ripple on the water to conceal our arrival from the trouties. And of course, as an apprentice, a ripple on the water helps as you tire, and tend to splash the cast of flies. In fact Campbell was in high hopes. He had carried the two new oars and my kit.

My portable rubber seat was a great success.

It was sufficiently wide to make it possible for me to turn one way or another without rubbing the side of my leg on the seat. After some time Campbell had me sit on the seat by his feet in the middle of the boat. I was afraid to do this as I thought my cast might whistle too close to his ears. He would hear nothing of that.

Well, I worked 'at the casting' all over the loch from about 12.30 'till 5 p.m., with a short break for lunch and we went up and down, across and back, pulling up and drifting, trailing the flies and casting in most square yards of the loch, at the place where the burn from the next loch comes in and the shallows at the narrows, over the deepest bit and even in the sheltered spot, but we did *not* raise one fish. All one sentence, just to emphasise the continuous concentration. Well, just like the job back home from 9.00 a.m. till 6.00 p.m. Never even saw one fish rise to the surface.

Campbell was ever full of optimism: "Oh, they are dour, these fish." "Never seen the like of it." "There's more fish came out of here than two or three other lochs put together." "Oh, I've seen some fine fish come out of this place" or "that place" as we fished over a particular spot. "Ye'll be getting tired. Don't do too much or ye'll tire your hand." "Oh, you're coming on with the casting. You're getting a long line out." "Oh, we'll smoke one out. We'll not get one at home." "Oh, you'll have had fine practice when the big fish comes." There's a lot of "Oh"s, but that's my Campbell.

All very supportive, we'd say today.

But three days and one trout was character building stuff to say the least and Campbell would only let me fish with the wind at my back. I got tired and twice caught the bank behind me, then ping, the fly was in my hat.

Then we did hear one plop in a quiet spot where the surface was like glass. When we rowed over to it the fish could have seen us 'miles away'.

During this time we saw two large birds fly by, black throated divers. They have bodies which are much thinner than domestic duck and a very long narrow neck which sticks out a long way. This particular variety has a white neck though the bird itself is a dark colour.

A cuckoo came flying over and stopped on the one tree in the neighbourhood, a stunted affair, on the shore. It let rip a bit of song. I'm not a cuckoo fancier. They lay their eggs in the nests of other birds for them to raise. But their call makes glad tidings that spring is here.

On the trek up and down I saw one lizard, about six inches long, and four frogs.

Campbell was not keen to hang about after eating his lunch as was noted by his remark after I approached him on the subject of his resting a little. "Oh," he says, "we're as well with the flies in the water as having them out of it."

Then I say: "What else can I do with this line of mine? I cast it all over the place." "Oh, you can't do more. They're just not taking. There's not a fish moving. That was a big fish we heard over there but it wouldn't take a fly."

So, I continue to question him on how to 'lure the beasties' on to my flies.

"Ah, it's all in the way you present the flies to the fish." Then he takes my rod and I see that he 'works the flies' rapidly through the water, pulling the line in quite quickly and locking the spare line under the right forefinger. Then he 'shoots all that spare line' when he casts.

So, into the fourth day. Seven lochs fished, one trout caught, pretty slow going.

A new plan of attack. I decided to give my rod

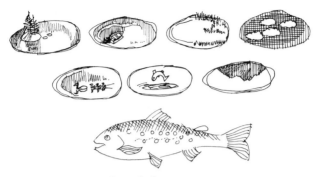

Seven lochs – one trout

to the ghillie quite a bit today. And I learned a lot. The line could be made to fly freely a long way, with the wind on your back. With an easy precise swing it could be made to shoot out nearly twenty feet. And, I could pull my cast off the water for the beginning of the casting movement while the flies were still in the water ten feet out. And I could have five feet of spare line ready to release. Not top professional stuff, but a great joy to me.

Campbell said I was getting my flies out just as far as him. The only difference was that he caught a trout of about 1 lb in weight.

I saw a heron today. It is a big grey bird with black tipped wings. It has a pinkish beak. It is very distinctive with its very long neck, long legs, very large wing span and exceedingly graceful flight.

Campbell spotted a golden eagle for me. We watched it for quite some time, floating about in slow flight, broad wings, fingered at the ends and each turned up.

For the fourth time Campbell said as we sat quietly on the bank eating lunch or changing the flies: "Fishing on a highland loch." Why he

27

says it I can't imagine. But that's the man, my counsellor, mentor, tutor. Always full of hope.

Perhaps I was being introduced to another dimension of life.

So, pay attention.

Below the surface was Campbell's understanding of nature and his accent on the range of feelings beginning to arise in my mind.

NOW WE MOVE ON TO CHARACTER BUILDING

DON'T take up fishing unless you believe in yourself. And character refining is a part of a ghillie's job.

The land in the West of Sutherland is very wild, very rough country. There is a remarkable amount of peat being cut near the road side. Also, I am surprised how much of the ground we cover is bog. It is mostly fairly firm under foot. Every now and then we pass over bits where the foot sinks. It is quite remarkable the number of places where a walking stick can be pushed straight down as far as it can go through the moss.

Today as we walked along in silence, Campbell suddenly stopped and surveyed the barren scene of square miles of wildness. Then he said: "I think this is the Deevil's own country, ups and downs and ups and downs and here and there a wee lochy. There's many a step I have taken here these past thirty years. In the old days there wasn't much fishing. It was all stalking ground here."

When we reached a loch, Campbell would prepare my rod and would add: "Now, take a seat for a bit before you start." After I've been flogging away at the water for two hours or more with him following me along the bank, he'd say: "Ah, you must be getting tired. They are dour these fish."

Then I'd call to him: "Come on guv'nor, what's wrong with what I'm doing?" "Ah, there's nothing wrong. You're getting on fine with the casting. You're doing all you can, the fish have to do their bit. We'll have to put some whisky on the flies."

So ended that day.

My Diary reads:

"The weather has been really March-like all the time I've been here. Only a little blink of sun. It really is like winter. Quite freezing – rain and icy winds every day."

Next morning, my sixth day with Campbell, he set off up the hill as usual at speed. I had changed my foot 'arrangements'. My long stockings plus my skiing stockings had been very comfortable on my left foot, but I had got a very painful spot between my little toe and next toe on my right foot. Today I tried wearing thin socks next my feet and long stockings over them. Much more room inside the boot now, though not quite so warm.

We rowed up to the top end of the loch and drifted back, me casting my line in all directions. There were flies on the water. They had floated up from the bottom (having emerged from the egg state) called nymphs. The fully grown flies emerge on the surface of the water, called duns. I collected two of them and put them in my collecting fluid. After mating the males and females are called spinners. Egg laying is different for different spinners. So there are three different forms of fly life which can be simulated to attract fish: Nymphs; Duns; Spinners.

But these fish took no notice of my duns, however smart they looked. So by one o'clock Campbell decided we'd better change to a different set of flies. The weather had gone cold and the water was much rougher. With these changes larger flies were called for. So we stopped for lunch.

As we were eating, local heifers passed on their way to the hills. They had already come about two miles up from the nearest croft and were quietly meandering away across the wilds unattended. Later in the day they had disappeared into a valley at least two miles further away from home. How on earth does the farmer find them and what a time it must take to fetch them home?

I noticed that Campbell's beer bottle had no cork. Then I recalled that when we started the day he had used it to cork the hole in the bottom of the boat, which of course has to be there to allow rain water through when the boat is pulled ashore. Yes, Campbell was for cold beer to drink. My flask had hot milk with lots of sugar – good when you are feeling cold.

By 2.30 p.m. I was really cold and decided I couldn't stick it any longer, so we rowed to the top of the loch and I got out to warm myself.

The hill by the loch goes up to 828 feet, so I set off up it. Just at the top I saw a fox. A great big animal, twice the size of a big cat. Its colour was rust brown. I got a close view of it.

Campbell stayed by the boat and we set off again.

By 4.00 p.m. I was so cold I decided I'd give up fishing altogether.

I told Campbell I wasn't very impressed with the fishing and that I had exhibited a good deal of patience all week with little result and he agreed. "There must be something wrong with the way I'm doing it," says I.

So came the character building bit from Campbell. Here was the point of decision. "The brown trout is a difficult fish. He will not rise unless he gets everything his own way. Conditions must be right before you get them. Now if it had been sea-trout or salmon they wouldn't have minded this cold weather, but not the trout. Oh yes, they have their own way."

Earlier in the day when we were getting nothing, he'd say: "Oh, the day is long." – meaning that there was plenty of time. "Oh yes, the fish have their time and nothing will budge them."

". . . there was a further dimension"

I suggested going to a neighbouring loch. To which Campbell replied: "Oh, you'd soon sour of fishing if you caught a lot every day." "Yes" he says, "I've been on this loch a thousand times

I'm sure. I've been here since I was at school." I then enquired how he got out on to the loch. "Oh, we had a big 18 foot bamboo pole for a rod and we used a worm and not a fly. And we'd fish at night, when the fish come to the side to feed in the evening."

So my lesson in philosophy continued as I listened to my Socrates.

Without saying much, Campbell challenged my attitudes. He introduced me to a new dimension. Behind his manner there was a sense of the Creator of that moorland and water. I was beginning to lose my sense of humour – a sure sign of stress.

Just as we were taking the last few drifts across the bottom end I got into a trout and away zipped the line off the reel.

It had taken my second fly (a Grouse and claret) and so my instruction in playing and landing a fish began again. Campbell kept talking all the time. The tension on the line was heavy and the rod was bent more than 90 degrees several times as the fish dashed about. It twice went under the boat, with Campbell shouting to me to sit at the back of the boat.

At one point we thought we could land it and I turned my rod point towards him. He lifted the landing net and got it caught in one of the rings on my rod. There was a moment of panic. No free line. It did tire in time and we landed a nice three-quarter pound trout. Campbell says I should have landed it in half the time. Says he won't tell me what to do next time, I can do it all myself.

Campbell is quite a fellow. Sometimes he nibbles and chews at black tobacco. A character as permanent as the hills around. Only, he is alive and has the antithesis of the grasshopper minds of so many city dwellers.

Campbell had a scientific approach in-built, which made it clear that flogging the water is a demonstration of ignorance of the width of understanding of nature. Quite unconsciously I was being confronted with my customary requirements for success. He was gently suggesting that nature is not something you can direct.

I had reached the critical point where success was the measure of my thinking. I had had to discover that there is a further dimension to be reached. And my philosophy professor had taken me through to wisdom.

I dissected my trout when I got home. I took out the stomach and floated off the contents in water. The fish had certainly been eating flies. There were plenty of them in its stomach along with all sorts of small flakes of vegetable matter. The flies, half digested, looked like little tadpoles.

Next morning I had it for breakfast. Fresh trout, boned and fried in butter with a touch of lemon. And I had caught it.

I described my trout post-mortem to the other fishers as we sat around the fire after dinner. Never a dull moment these occasions. One lady fell into a loch today. She was fully immersed, then lost her way on the moors and went miles out of her way. Fortunately she found the road and was picked up. Then we had an account of the end of the grocer's van. It had gone over the edge and rolled down a vast hillside. All that was left was the chassis in one piece and the rest of it in bits in a mixture of fruit, biscuits, jam and sundry ill-defined broken boxes. The driver only got a few bruises. Someone else capped that one with the story of the local district nurse who did the same a few days earlier. She was driving next day.

2
Companion and Luminary

ROBBIE ROSS OF
SUTHERLAND AND HIS
WORLD

I HAD graduated from the care of Campbell, my first Tutor in Sutherland and acquired a new ghillie, Robbie Ross, young and athletic.

The first day we made a tour of six lochs but caught nothing. Landing a fly on a glass-like surface was still beyond me so we moved to a large loch which had a boat. Along one side the bank went straight up very steeply. It was correspondingly deep there. There were only just two trees on the landscape. It would be difficult to describe them. They were only just trees, well worn by the winds and weather. All of a sudden I caught something. But it was up behind me and there was my tackle and hooks up in one tree and the boat drifting away at a fair pace. Ross turned the boat while I let out the line to avoid breaking the leader. The tree was out at 45° over the loch. It looked half rotten so I kept the boat under it in case it broke. The boat began to stray in the wind with me in it alone. He had not yet loosened the line and leader. I lost an oar overboard and it began to float away. I made a stroke at it with the one remaining oar and managed to drag it back, rowed back to the tree too fast and nearly broke the other rod which was protruding over the bow.

Ross stayed up the tree while I photographed him suspended in mid air. It was the only funny incident of the day.

I was feeling very fit even though we were soaked after heavy showers of rain. It is four

miles over the hills from this loch to the road.
We went down in one hour and two minutes,
just like the old mountaineering days when
those who were in a hurry for a hot bath just
crashed through the bogs and all.

Each day I went fishing on the lochs under
Ben Foinaven and Ben Arkle, I looked up at
those mountains with a faint hope that one day
I would have enough energy to climb them. It
isn't altogether the energy, but in addition
these Bens are well back from the road.

The loch which nestles in the deepest part of the horse-shoe curve of the various tops of these two mountains is three hours' rough walking over the hills.

Roughly then, our plan of action for climbing would be to climb Foinaven from the shoulder nearest the road, walk along the ridge of Foinaven, over the three main tops and come down a great stone gully just opposite our target loch. Fish some of the smaller lochs and so back to the road by traversing the lower slopes of Foinaven.

We drove down four miles and fortunately we discovered that the local policeman was going out to dig peat, and we got a lift from him for another two miles. We left the roadside about 10 a.m. and got back at 7 p.m. – nine hours on the hills.

It was a warm day so left most of my mountaineering clothes with the policeman and Robbie planted his beer bottle down in a culvert under the road to keep it cool.

We had a long walk over slowly rising bog and heather. The mountain lambs are fine beasts according to Robbie. But a goodly number get lost because there is no one to shepherd them. They are out alone for two to three months.

At various places on the high ground, the moss and heather grow right across the little burns and here and there are holes which go down to the burn. One can hear the burn though one cannot see it. The hole may look like an oversized rabbit hole. If a lamb goes down, nothing can get it out short of human help which is far away.

Ross had been over Foinaven several times a year, shepherding and stalking. Half way up we left the heather and the crackle of last autumn twigs under foot. Ross thought it was the first time a fishing rod had been carried over these mountains.

We found a pipit's nest with three eggs. It looked cosy in the bank of bog tussock. We spotted a great brown hare loping across the hillside. It wasn't moving fast. Probably had young in some snug corner nearby.

In two hours and a quarter we reached the first of our tops. There were fine views: round to the North of Scotland to the headland away beyond the Kyle of Tongue and out to the island of Lewis in the Hebrides, then down the West coast. There were no clouds, just some heat haze, a view of nearly fifty miles radius.

We were ready for our sandwiches and coffee, before setting off along the narrow shoulder which connects this with the other tops.

There are some terrific rock faces. They look like iron, rough and knotted as a piece of clinker out of a fire. There were other pieces of quartzite which had rings all of even size punched into them. Fossil markings may be. There is one particularly fine buttress which runs out to the North East. This North side of Foinaven would make some great snow climbs. There are a variety of gradients for 1,000 feet, open faces, deep gullies with big rocks for difficult climbs. It has now been found by the mountaineering fraternity.

We started to descend beyond the third top, down one of those screes of stones. At the top the little rocks consist of pieces as small as grains of sand, with some as big as a hen's egg. I sank in over my boot tops, but soon learned to let gravity get on with it. The angle of the scree must have been nearly one in two. It was one long slide leaning far back, sometimes on one leg sometimes on both. Stones flew off like

snowflakes. A few hundred feet in just a few moments. Suddenly there is a 'thin' spot. Here there is a rock down underneath and the surface collection of stones is not thick. I had been leaning too far back and went down with a bump or just managed to rebalance with a

A thousand foot scree

jump. We were soon down a thousand feet to reach a mixture of rock, moss and heather. And of course I had been protecting my precious fishing rod.

Progress ceased altogether. For the first time it was steep and yet very rough. My ankles began to complain. The boulders were now as large as a bowler hat. In the midst of this high scree one may come across a well beaten track, just about eight inches wide, which has been trodden down over the years by the deer. It was a welcome relief to get on to one of these deer tracks and traverse sideways across the mountain. The lower part of the scree, with its still steep inclination and its big broken rocks and moss was the most tiring part of the descent.

Beginner's Paradise

We got down to the first lochan, ate the rest of our food and started to fish. One rises to the occasion, casts a beautiful line and 'ping' there is a fish on. Small, of course, but one learns how to handle all the slack line in the left hand. I had two trout on my line at the same time on one occasion. We carried no landing net so had to beach the fish.

I caught four and Ross took the rod and caught three. We put them all back.

Two on at the same time

This lochan had not been fished for years, so possibly the fish had never seen an artificial fly.

The day was warm. We stayed just three quarters of an hour. Ross at times could not finish lunch for my calls to come and unhook a fish. We moved off to another larger loch about 4 p.m.

I took off my boots, socks and trousers, rolled up my long underpants, put my boots back on again to protect my 'city' feet and waded out at the mouth of a burn running into the loch. Caught three better trout and kept them.

It was the last week of May and the ferns were just about eight or ten inches high. The leaf was just forming. It was very green with that tight whorl at the tip. May is the special month for admiring ferns.

We left the loch at 5.30 p.m. and went at full tilt over the moors, straight through the bogs to the road. This we achieved in one and a half hours. Just like a graduate from University, Robbie had joyous expectations. He was ready to do what any ambitious post-graduate student would do – roam the hills, talk about the vast scenario of geological formations, animals, birds and return to his love of the job and teaching his guest to fish.

That's what makes ghillies, ghillies.

It had been the best combination of fishing and mountaineering.

STORM AND TRANQUILLITY
BY THE LOCHAN

THERE is no fishing on Sundays in the far
North, so I went off to Church. Gaelic
service at 12.0 noon, English at 1.0 p.m. It was a
very 'deep in the country' service. About thirty
in the congregation. We sat to sing and stood to
pray. There was a Presenter, no organ (and the
rustle of paper as various people prepared to eat
sweets during the sermon). The minister had
been there for 44 years. His text: "Except the
Lord build the house, the labourers labour in
vain."

We sang the 50th Psalm:
"The mighty God, even our Lord,
    hath spoken, and called the earth
from the rising of the sun unto the
    going down thereof."
And the 100th Psalm:
"Make a joyous noise unto the Lord
    all ye lands.
Serve the Lord with gladness; come before
    his presence with singing."
I had to leave before a christening as someone
was coming to pick me up, then off to tea with
the Ross family.

Next day Robbie and I were off again very
early; five miles by car then a mile and a
quarter up the river bank to the high ground
near its origin. Then on up the steep incline of
the hillside and a further two miles over the
hills and moors. There is a very wide burn to
cross with 40 or more steps to be taken on the
stones to get across. Must be very difficult at

times of spate. So, into a boat and one mile to the far end.

Fishing began at 11.30 a.m. and in one hour I had four trout – an all time record for me.

The weather began to look peculiar. The wind would stop altogether, then it would start again and blow the opposite way. Then Ross said: "The fish are going down because they feel the rain coming." There was not only rain coming, there was a summer thunder storm on its way. The wind had gone again completely so we trailed 30 feet of line as we headed for the shore and we got a fish, the first I had had trailing a fly. I wound in furiously as the fish chose to swim toward the boat. Suddenly there was no tension on the line. I had lost my fish.

The whole sky to the South and East was low and black and there was a distant rumble of thunder. Robbie decided we should stop and find shelter under a high cliff in a cave with a big overhanging top from which we could watch the thunder storm.

Someone later described it as "God's own ordnance" and it was like the thunder of guns rumbling around the heavens.

There were big vertical flashes of lightning, then rain and hailstones. The black clouds hurtled up the sky from the South East like a black volcano belching. At a lower level another wispy torn cloud rushed in a direction almost at right angles from West to East. Later there was to be seen a magnificent white billowy cloud right away behind the storm and much higher in the heavens, beside a patch of blue sky.

During the hailstorm the surface of the loch was marked like a very fine grain sand paper or grater. It was a fine sight.

The majesty of that spectacular thunder-storm was the stuff of Robbie's experience. It

"God's own ordnance"

had taught him to respect the heavens as he had learned to respect the moorlands and the mountains.

We were snug and dry in our cave well up on the hillside and had a Grand Stand view of the storm moving out to the North West, ten or more miles away. Peculiar too, the storm did not break around our ears but happened at about 3,000 feet, so we could see through all the rain and hail for miles.

We put on another cast while up in our dent in the rocks and it was just as well, because after the storm there was a dead calm. The trout were rising in all directions, little ones near the shore, big ones far out.

Ross couldn't resist it. Neither could I.

So we went trailing our flies down the deep part of the loch and sure enough we struck a fish. The line went singing off the reel with that song which is music to the fisherman. The bend on the rod suggested a good fish. Suddenly it jumped out of the water about twenty feet behind the boat. It seemed strange because the line was drooping straight back to a point under the water. It was one of these quick flashes of puzzlement, that didn't convey anything to me. I soon discovered that there were two fish on the tackle. The big one had jumped. It was on the end or tail fly. The smaller fish was under water on the second dropper.

There was a lot of to-ing and fro-ing. I changed my seat from the back of the boat to the spare one in the middle so I could watch, keep the right tension on the line and so forth.

Ross landed both fish with his net, without breaking the cast.

They were half pounders.

It is good to see a ghillie laugh. On one occasion we were both helpless with laughter so that the tears all but rolled down our cheeks.

I had got into a good fish when it rushed towards me. I was standing on some rocks with Ross by my side. I whipped up the rod point over my shoulder and started to reel in. It was of little avail, the slack on my line was VAST, so I grabbed the line near the butt of the rod and heaved at that. Not enough, so I grabbed the line in front of my nose. What would have happened if the fish had turned, I can't guess. It was finally landed by the method one sees being used by little boys off a South coast pier.

It was 'one of those days'. I lost as many as I caught. Six of the fifteen I took home were nice fish. And with the aid of a few from the baskets of other residents at the Hotel I was able to send down a box to the practice in London. Each was rolled separately with sandwich paper, tied with string and labelled with the name of the recipient. Everyone of the staff got one.

Ross had the rod for a time and as he fished I learned more about handling spare line. He caught some and my Number Two Tutor seemed satisfied with my performance.

ROBBIE ROSS'S BIRDS BY THE WATER

OUR hours of walking and climbing over the moors and up the mountains were no drudgery. Robbie had comment to make continuously. He treated me to his enthusiasm for everything. No bird was too insignificant for him to tell me about.

Today there were four birds. The stonechat is a little bird which is a mixture between a chaffinch and a robin. It has a black head with a distinct white band round its forehead. It has almost a red breast. A pretty bird at this grey time of the year and spring just on the move.

The next was a raven. It is a big edition of the crow. The body looks more torpedo shaped and flaps its wings more slowly over the mountains. It has a massive bill and a wedge-shaped tail.

The oyster-catcher is as distinctive as the magpie. We have seen quite a few of these oyster-catchers with their long orange coloured legs and a long orange coloured beak. The wings are like aeroplane wings, the leading edge is black and the back edge is white. Each wing is black and white from tip to tip in contrast with the magpie which has a black tip and white base to each wing. These oyster-catchers have white heads. They look like black and white balls as they sit on the water.

The fourth bird was the sandpiper. There are plenty of them. All I could record was that it was a medium sized bird which flies fast and its wings make a long sweep from the highest to the lowest point. The bird is greyish and brown.

There are eleven different sandpipers in my Birdwatcher's Book.

Each day brings its surprise. Today it is a blackcock, which supplies the feathers on the Glengarry bonnet. The tail of the bird is split and it is this which makes the distinctive decoration for the hat. Its proper name is black grouse.

I had a much closer view of the grouse and the buzzard this day as well. The buzzard is a really big bird. Its eyesight is eight times keener than man's.

Yet another day we found a meadow pipit's nest, with a clutch of five eggs in it. Little dark grey eggs almost the size of my thumb nail. The eggs were almost black at the broad round end. We were able to return to this nest when the bird was sitting. It is a nice little bird with a very sharp face and small dark beak. Little black eyes with small rings of white feathers around each peer out at you. The general colour is dark grey and brown. There is a very distinct white patch of feathers in its tail which you can see when it flies. Its wings go through a long sweep up and down, and it flies fast. 'A born victim', the pipit, a favourite host for the cuckoo. The pipit sometimes stands on the back of its huge foster-child to feed it.

There is always something new to see at your favoured place in the hills. We have one we hope to visit in the last weeks of June or early in July each year. There has always been something magic about it these past years.

One lochan nestles in a very small dip between high hills. It has no glen of its own. It is just the size of two tennis courts. Along one side and along one end is another area about the same size with broken ground, slips of water, tall grasses, little flat tops of turf just big enough for a very flat nest of dried reeds.

When we approach, still nearly quarter of a mile away, the 'sentinel birds' are flying over our head wanting to know what we are doing there. As we crest the nearby shoulder of the hill, still 400 yards from the lochan, up will fly fifty father and mother black-headed gulls.

It is a dramatic sight these gulls flurrying vertically over their homes, squawking and whirling, seen against the dark brown of last year's heather and fresh patches of pale mustard-coloured ferns just a few weeks old, with their tops still curled tight.

It is an unbelievable sight as it breaks in front of you.

If we stop moving, the birds settle down again almost immediately, some landing on the lochan. So we move cautiously round to a high bank on the left still 300 yards from the lochan and this movement puts up the whole five hundred or more.

Stop again and get the binoculars out. There below us are nests with their dark chocolate-blotched camouflaged eggs.

Soon they are all, well nearly all, settled down again.

As it flies one sees the other marker on this bird. It is the white leading edge to the outer wing feathers.

The Diary reads:

30th May	– many hens sitting.
24th June	– sixteen gulls on the lochan – fluffy balls.
29th June	– thirtytwo gulls – fluffy balls.
28th July	– eight half grown gulls swimming on the lochan.

A WARNING TO BEGINNERS LIKE ME

THE joy of getting off to the streams and lochans is fine. It is easy to think we know enough. I was still a rat-racer of limited liability scholarship from a background of professional men who think they are all prima donnas.

So, how to find the right place to fish?

As in so many departments of life, a good reputation is built by those who constantly produce the goods. Fishing centres appear to be no exception and it is wise to be guided by those who know. There is always the fishing tackle proprietor. He will have inside knowledge of where fish are to be found, what fish and at what season. He will know if ghillies are to hand.

I didn't want to be organised, I thought. So I did not ask my fishing tackle guide in Inverness. I was too busy on the job and finally answered an advertisement in The Times, London. Good paper as it usually is, there is no guarantee that quality goods are being advertised. I rose to a splendid 'fly'. I won't even

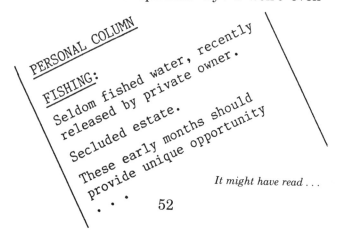

PERSONAL COLUMN

FISHING: Seldom fished water, recently released by private owner. Secluded estate. These early months should provide unique opportunity . . .

It might have read . . .

52

reveal which of the islands off the West Coast of Scotland it happened on because I like that part of the country too much to damn the rest of the fishing.

Up till then I had been a rod borrower as well as a duffer at fishing. I had inherited flies, mostly 'cast-offs' of experienced fishermen. Incidentally, others who have looked at them since, have done so with 'goggle-eyes' because I have a good collection of fine trout flies, sea-trout and a few salmon flies.

My preparations had been rather precipitate in the three weeks prior to this break. I had made a resolution to keep my fishing 'things' together, but I had moved house twice, so the same old fuss started. I boarded the night train for Scotland with six or seven pieces of baggage. I kept a firm grip on my precious borrowed rods.

There is something about travelling to fish which should be recommended in the daily routine of life. I had three conversations going North. One in the Guards Van with the owner of two whippets; one with a young couple going on holiday to take photographs (at least the husband was); and one with two fellow fishermen. I did one dental operation on the Head-waiter of the Restaurant Car and I met a chap I had not seen for twelve years.

I spent nearly half an hour with the whippet man and learned quite a bit about how dog racing is classified. How to make dogs run slow or fast, with appropriate meals, vaseline on the forehead which runs into the eyes when the dog perspires (perhaps he was having me on, but fun just the same), training to kill live rabbits to give them the urge to chase and kill the hare at the greyhound stadium and so on. He assured me that it is impossible for the public to tell which dog will win by looking at the dog's performance on any track, except the nationally controlled tracks.

And so to my island.

I arrived and was a little dashed to find that I was not met by 'mine host'. As I was driven back to 'this place in the highlands' by two lady guests (the only two) staying there, I realised that I was being given an orientation talk on what I was likely to find. "He", was away in London. "She" had lost the only two staff she had. There were no men around the estate except the gamekeeper who really belonged to the man who owned the whole island and so on and on. As we passed into the house grounds I soon realised that 'the river' was only a big burn (very small stream) and that everything else had been likewise exaggerated.

It transpired that there were no ghillies, no motor transport, 'the river' became a river only when there was a spate, and then only lasted in that state for a very short time because it only had a small catchment area. "She" was doing her best, I could see. The food was fine considering that "he" had not given "her" any money to pay the shop (seven miles away) for so many weeks that food supplies had been stopped. They were not local people. They had taken the place on a fourteen year lease, a year ago.

It was not only a source of grief to me and to other guests who had come and been disappointed, but to the local countryside as well. To make a sporting centre 'go', there needs to be someone to make it go and 'mine host' was off on business elsewhere and there was more to the story, but enough.

It took a good deal of courage for me, a mere beginner at fishing, to say that they had misrepresented their estate. The two ladies who met me drove me away inside twentyfour hours.

And so, after several long distance telephone calls to my Inverness 'tackle man' and 'new quarters arranged', I left the island. I had arrived on Friday and had to move rapidly on Saturday, because you cannot do any removing by public transport on Sunday in the West Highlands, which is a good thing.

And so to Invergarry Hotel on the Caledonian Canal, south of Inverness.

A fine river, the Garry, runs under my window. The hillside, over the way, is a blaze of rhododendron in full flower. Where there is a space on the ground, it is covered with a blanket of bluebells. The broom seems more startlingly yellow than I've ever seen it. The lupins are on the way.

And I have John Macaskill as my ghillie.

JOHN MACASKILL OF INVERNESS – GHILLIE EXTRAORDINARY

IT is a bit difficult to describe the sensation of fishing for the first time on a fast flowing highland river. I did not really know if I could cast the fly properly to put it exactly where I wanted it. There are the trees, the big rugged rocks and and the wind.

It is more than four miles down the Garry to

Loch Oich (Caledonian Canal). The river twists and turns gathering water and momentum all the way. It rushes crashing over falls. There are deep black gullies where it moves like a mill race. There are many signs high up the banks marking former spring spates. Great logs and fallen trees lie there six feet and more from the water edge.

But I had John Macaskill by me. His presence was very real. There he was, with his sure foot, moving from rock to rock, showing me how to cast right hand and left hand. By the time I had been there a few days I had to record his character in a poem . . .

John Macaskill – ghillie extraordinary

There's a stalky lad, a Lovat Scout
    That you should get to know.
Professor Piscatores moves fast on spritely
toe.
    His bunnet's like a bee's bike
With flies you ought to know
    If in the river Garry a fishing you would
go.

His lower jaw sticks out a bit
    His nose it steers the show
A day out with Macaskill
    Ye'll aye be on the go.
Starting at the Falls in
    The fast runs down below
As it scurries 'round the boulders
    Black pots of swirl and flow.

His tweeds they match the river side,
    His jacket, breeks and hose,
Ye'll learn to 'ghost', be 'not around'
    And seldom the fish knows
There's a man behind the fly there
    That swims above its nose.

He's a master of the art
    Of retrieving flies from trees.
I was only caught up twice
    As I hoped the 'Prof' to please.
Then after him I'd boulder jump,
    I hoped my nails would seize.
I've seen him on a boulder
    Water half up to his knees.

He's a man of great endurance
    With the likes of those
Who fankle up their cast of flies –
    Or when midgies through his hose
Eat all day long his shin bones
    His patience never goes.

"No striking at the fish", he'll say.
  "The tension does the trick."
"If you'll keep your flies aye fishing –
  There'll be no need – strike quick.
"Keep it in the water right up to the net –
  Or you'll soon know how much power's
    in a trout's tail flick."

As he takes you down the river
  From run to pool you go
Sometimes in the middle rush
  Rarely in the slow.
Under banks and over rocks
  Your friends would never know
Macaskill's duffer pupil's
Learning trouting, awful slow.

With John below the Falls of Garry

There on your right almost above your head the power-house of the Garry Falls. It is a moving experience to stand on a great grey rock out below the falls with the cauldron boiling round, a great roar in the ears, a faint breeze in the face and a grey sky overhead.

I cast into the foam and let the flies come around into the still water behind the massive boulders.

A rod length away under the high cliff was John with the landing net, full of hope. He was there too to disentangle my flies if they got caught on the rocks or I tangle the line itself in my excitement. I was participating in the most exciting adventure – fishing a wild-running highland river.

To get to that rock I had had to creep along under the cliff – jumping from rock to rock. No,

Below the Falls of Garry

I did not do much moving around after I had got there. I was there – at the heart of 'the action'.

On one occasion I had been using a short line and had just begun to throw a longer one when I got into a trout. I immediately straightened up to get some tension on the line, but I had had too much slack and I could not strike and he was off and away.

After a shower of rain the air by the river is exotic. This is not just the fragrance of wild flowers, there is a 'fresh off the ice' tang about it, like the winter breezes in Southern California. The intoxication doesn't go to your head but it feels good.

I discovered that carrying the rod the proper way – butt first, resulted in my becoming caught on bushes, ferns and fir trees behind me. I learned to walk point first, just as long as I reversed, to butt first, climbing down the rocks.

Back on my rock. Give the flies time to come round themselves and they are more likely to stay under the water and stay off other rocks. Work the flies and they will remain on top. I saw a trout jump out of the water right over the spot where my flies were likely to be. One explanation is that in taking a fly a fish may want to come down on top of it.

So different from fishing a lochan.

There are many occasions when having cast the fly on the water over a rising fish I have seen another rise just where my fly ought to be. There would be a swirl on the water surface. Now I felt nothing on my rod. I used to think the fish was just 'having a look'. I an now informed that the fish can take a fly in its mouth and put it out again so fast you will not feel anything on the line.

One has to – 'Strike the rise'!

And we did and had fish.

BY THE RIVER GARRY IN JUNE

A glen amid the mountain air
　clothed in green and brown.
Birch and fir are everywhere,
　but not too close to drown
The beauty of the riotous fair
　rhododendrons that abound.

For mile on mile – in equal share
　purple clumps mid green and brown.
Tree-like banks their state declare,
　their massed trumpets ought to drown
The hill and rush of Garry there
　a ceaseless mighty sound.

After a shower, fresh is the air
　and massive carpets of bloom are found
By salmon pool and trouty lair,
　o'er moss and bracken everywhere
A sight, some searching to compare
　these paths by Garry, winding round.

These silent blooms, built with such care,
　have been here the decades down.
Great billowy masses, we fall heir
　each Spring as country calls to town
To witness this – not man's affair,
　and be glad – 'to be around'.

ONE goes on being lifted by the whole emphasis on Spring.

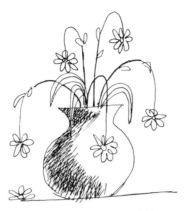

. . . sad flowers next morning

Eight varieties of wild flower in two square feet is a not unusual sight on the river bank, a brilliant mix of colour.

It is virtually impossible to fish by some streams without damaging wild flowers. Don't leave them there to die. Take them home. No, they need not be all dead by morning, you will be pleased to know there is an answer. If possible find a few docken leaves which are broad, to wrap around the actual hand-hold area of your bundle. The bluebells, cow parsley, herb Robert may all look rather bedraggled by the time they reach home.

Put the bunch in a vase and empty in a tin of lemonade and top this up with plain water. If there is a carbonating machine in the kitchen, plain water carbonated does exactly the same at less cost.

The bluebells will return to their erect stature of the river bank. Our herb Robert grew six inches in six days in these conditions. What's more, shop purchased carnations can last three weeks.

Two birches across the Dog Pool

SHOPPING FOR MY FIRST ROD

MY Inverness fishing tackle shop proprietor had rescued me when in my ignorance I went to fish on the strength of a Trade Advertisement, which proved to be a non-starter. So, to him I went for advice on buying a rod.

The display of rods was overwhelming. It was not quite like buying a motor car. There are simple questions for car purchase.

With rods there was a confusion of marginal refinement, delicacy, shade of difference, nuance, or so it seemed to me. And, a balancing line.

A few inches longer or shorter; three piece with a spare top; quick recoil; firmer action; good looks – Oh dear!

Yes, I guess you get what you pay for and after all he had rescued me, so he should know. "He is asking me where I am going to fish. Gosh, where am I going to fish?"

Take the one he suggests. And a metal case to protect it.

Where shall I start to buy a rod?
  A different kind has ilka bod.
They all have points that they would say
  ye maun hae in a good fly rod

So, search on for yer rod.

Where shall I start to buy a rod?
  when long and short are just as good
I 'wheech aroun' as each I hand
  I dinna ken, but I just nod,

As I search on for my rod.

Where shall I start to buy my rod?
    The supple kind or girth right broad?
Glass, split-cane or metaloid?
    the choice is vast for one as void

of clues in searching for his rod.

Where shall I start to buy a rod?
    Some streams are narrow and some
    broad,
chalk streams and mountain ye'll hae trod
    as after trout you steady plod

so search ye well for that new rod.

Now I have bought my first trout rod,
    no broomstick it or builders' hod,
light's a feather and balance good
    It's got a case lest any should
disrespect this crafted wood
    nine feet long and tidy shod
split cane and tapered line and I would

say – the next thing now is "use the rod!"

TEN LESSONS FROM
JOHN McINTYRE

THERE are so many things to see around the banks of a river or loch that John, with his gentle yet firm approach, got on with the capture of my mind. He was ghillie, stalker, road mender, gardener, companion, teacher of life-science. He understood human nature.

His short interruptions of my straying mind brought me to heel. Out of the blue he would sum up the situation and I had to pay attention – THUS:

1. *"Now pay attention to your business and no more photographs."*
'Discipline is what you need'. He had come to fish. Well, he might not have understood that the scene was so breathtaking I wanted to remember it.

2. *"It will be lowsin' time by the time ye get started."*
He was recalling the days when ploughs were pulled by horses. After a long day the horses would be loosened (lowsed) from the chains and halter pulling the plough, to go back to the farm. You might think that a gentleman of the hills would proceed with seemliness (a speed suited to the occasion); no hurry. John had prepared the scene of our adventure, so 'don't you hang about.'

3. *"I'll take you to where the fish are – you'll have to catch them."*

That's the sort of support to give those you have charge of. I've opened the door. You walk in.

4. *"Oh! I like going out with someone who doesn't want a hundred fish."*
That's the speed of and richness of life with the man of the moors and the lochans. It slows you down, and you need that. You take time for friendship.

5. *"Now mind ye don't tramp on ma' flees!"*
I was moving about the boat not taking due care of John's plan of attack. 'More discipline please.'

6. *"Ye're an awful man to go out with – no matches!"*
Yes, the friendship of two whose lives are normally poles apart is refreshing.

7. *"You'll need to nip them faster."*
'But, don't get lazy while we are enjoying the peace and tranquillity of the lochan and the mountains.'

8. *"That's the time to fish – a rising river and a falling loch."*

9. *"Bright day – bright fly. Dull day – dull fly."*
Fishing techniques have basic principles, just as yours do. So 'learn your lines!'

10. *"In my humble opinion, if the fish are taking the fly they'll take anything and if they are not and are lying on the bottom sulking, not even the devil will move them."*
(Said with the proper Scots accent)

There are some basic rules about life. You have to get to know your 'patient', 'client', 'quarry', 'fish'. But far more, you are obliged to study the world they/we live in, or you spend an awful lot of time and money exhausting yourself and just being ineffective. Could there be a message in this for those who claim to lead?

"In my humble opinion . . ."

There was genuine friendship in the man. He wanted me to maintain perspective. I relaxed to the point where I began to do some sketching by the river bank.

Pearls from the Wisdom of John McIntyre

There's fish all over every loch,
  but there's a fact quite clear
There's a spot behind an island
  or a bay – a thoroughfare.

If the fish are on the move
  there's many a fly will do –
Peter Ross, Grouse and Green –
  to mention only two.

If they're lying on the bottom
  a-sulking there below
The deil himsel' won't move them
  you'll be tired afore ye go.

It's good to know the depth of water
  underneath your boat
After two fish lost in weeds
  you'll be wiser than a stoat.

Trail the flies well out behind
  when going up to drift.
Somedays you'll get the largest trout
  as though it was a gift.

When the loch has risen
  moss, heather banks, submerge
New source of food available
  larger trout emerge.

In a fast running river
  the tension does the trick.
When you're drifting on a windless loch
  you have to nip them quick.

Keep your eye on the water
  don't gaze around
He'll take the fly and throw it out
  you'll only hear the sound.

When the river is rising,
  is the best time to choose.
New and enticing things
  come past the trouties' nose.

A loch that's going down
  is a good place to try.
He's losing these fresh banks
  will pay attention to a fly.

You've got to keep on fishing
  with your mind on that alone
Photos, sketching, dreaming –
  John McIntyre he'll groan.

But let the day out fishing
  be all that one could wish
Don't let it get too serious
  or want a hundred fish.

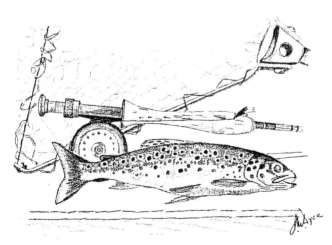

A Garry trout

71

3
Character Building

"YOU'RE NO' A PURIST ARE YOU?" SAYS SEUMAS ON THE ORCHY, ARGYLL

I HAD fished for five days on the river Dee in Aberdeenshire, at a splendid stretch beside Crathes Castle. I was using my new two-handed salmon fly rod. The owner encouraged me in my pursuit of the salmon. The ghillie taught me to Spey Cast. Well, I did get two sea trout and the picnic provided was delicious.

My wife and I moved on to the West of Scotland to another patient who invited us to stay at her lodge and fish her water on the river Orchy by Dalmally.

The first morning I was met outside the lodge by the Head Keeper, with his Land Rover bedecked with rods. I tentatively showed him the flies I had been using on the Dee. His professional eye showed approval but he suggested, if I didn't mind, we might do a bit of spinning for salmon.

We drove up the Orchy. It has the most splendid pools I've seen. Seumas (the ghillie) selected an idyllic pool. The water was deep. It was moving quite fast.

Said Seumas: "We'll just spin down this pool and if we don't raise anything we'll just put on the wurrm."

He was looking at me straight in the eye at a distance of about two feet. The shock within me was immediate. I had just been the guest of another patient whose home was by the Test in Hampshire. To me, there was no other lure for the game fish than a fly, landing delicately and precisely on the water. And I had been lectured by my ghillie in a boat on a highland loch, who saw I was too slow in my strike. These lochan trout can take a fly and spit it out before there is a noticeable impulse for your response. When you are in the care of a highland ghillie, his comment is likely to be the one hurled at me on occasion: "Well, I canna' do mair than pit you over the fush!"

And here was someone suggesting I go for a salmon with "the wurrm".

Within a split second Seumas followed his offering: "You're no' a purist are you?"

He had sized me up within a few moments of our first meeting. I had already put myself in a class of fisherman, quite unconciously. He was telling me there are no classes. There are no unsporting methods, only unsporting fishermen. That was the dimension of the man's mind, which had immediate implications beyond the job on hand. Looking back, Seumas was saying: "You may be special, but so is everyone else."

What was I to say? "There's a lot of ways of killing a fish and I'm here to learn. You tell me what to do" says I.

Well, it was a precise and accurate system. I had an eleven pound salmon on that 8th. day of June 1972.

Oh! You want to know how it is done?

Collect some nice fresh lob worms. Keep them in a tin in wet moss. Put five or six long juicy ones on the hook.

Cast the 'lure' right across the river and keep the rod point exactly in line with the spot where the cluster of worms lands on the water. The cluster must hit the water as though it had just fallen off the branch of a tree overhead. As natural as possible. At that moment pull off

74

about two feet of line with the left hand and hold it there out to the left of the body. Don't move the rod.

The line will begin to swing in an arc with the current in the water. It will arrive on your own side down stream. Don't move. Your rod is still pointing in its original direction. Your line is straight down your bank.

I had been told by Seumas to stay like that, in silence. "If a fish (salmon) is interested you will feel a distinct 'dunt' on your line. Don't move the rod."

So, how long do you stand the awaiting 'a dunt'? A very long time.

Seumas told me to try again. I did. The third interminable time – then 'dunt'! When that happens, let go the line held in the left hand. Don't move the rod. Pull off a further two feet, hold it, stay silent.

There is an electric sensation through the body as the words "a fish" are muttered around. I let go my two feet of line with 'the dunt', pulled off the next two feet, held it, stayed silent and wondered what was going to happen next.

After an interminable period of growing excitement came another 'dunt'. I let go my two feet of line again and plucked off two more from the reel.

I could see nothing suggesting hope in the water. Perhaps the first 'dunt' was just the line becoming snarled on a boulder as the current tried to carry the line down the stream with it. But a second precise 'dunt' was surely more significant. I was by this time a bit worried. My rod was still pointing across the river. My line down the river. Just about anything might happen.

There came the third 'dunt'. I was convinced there was activity down below. Still no movement I could see or feel. I let go my two feet of line.

How long should I stay immobilised? How long could my excitement be held in check? No longer!

I lifted the rod point slowly. It was still pointing across the river. Then something astonishing began to happen. The line, still straight from the rod point, appeared to be moving slowly across the river. "Ye Gods it is a fish! And it's moving – deep down."

Thereafter, everything happened. The fish moved fast. My reel screamed. The salmon leapt out of the water. I moved back up the bank to help take up the slack on my line. As the fish rushed towards me and my line went slack I wound the reel at breakneck speed. All went quiet for a bit. Then the whole process again and again. Forward and backward I went, keeping my line tight enough but loose enough to let the fish fly when it chose. As time went by I was able to tighten on the fish though ready to let him go if he must.

As Seumas explained later: "You can't strike a salmon when it takes its first nibble at the worm. It has to have the 'lure' well down its throat or you won't hold it."

Next day my wife was in the local store, which sells everything. The proprietor knew I had been out the day before. They usually do. She asked if I had had any luck. "Yes", says my wife: "He had an eleven pound salmon."

"And what did he get it on?" says the store keeper.

For a split second my wife was as baffled as I, with my 'purist' outlook the day before. But before her embarrassment could show, the proprietor chipped in: "Oh yes, a garden fly."

But this is not a story to tell to the purist. One

has to be mindful of one's audience. The fish was duly laid out on drawer-lining paper and outlined, photographed and so forth. All of which were later framed.

A FURTHER WARNING AND
THE CONTRAST OF A DAY
WITH WILLY ON LOCH TAY

IF you want an intensive post-graduate semi-nar, go where the knowledge is.

If you want to learn quickly how to handle, hold, play, land a salmon, go where the reputation is.

So, let's book into a Hotel on the river Tweed in Scotland. There will be lots of salmon and we can learn faster.

This time, my wife and I were joined by a senior consultant physician. Reg was older and wiser than I and I laid on this epic fishing.

After dinner we went for a walk to the river. We had booked our rods (the fishing way of saying we had known stretches of the river bank) for next morning.

There was the Tweed of great renown. Just the place to be, and a 'conversation piece' on our return South. It was wide, moving majestically as it had done for centuries, through lowland agricultural and heathland country. We experienced that mixture of respect, a growing feeling of a hunt for booty and a prestigious prize.

"But, what are these?"

Right alongside our bank were very large rowing boats, containing large heaps of nets. "What's going on here?"

Yes, the beats we had booked to fish had just been netted. Our Tweed dream was shattered.

Well, if there is one thing to learn for successful clinical practice, it is to face facts, not dreams. Back at the Hotel we challenged the Management, stayed the night and left in the

Salmon netting

morning. I looked around the breakfast room that morning and spotted a solitary tweedy gent. "Yes, there is no good salmon fishing here. I have the Brednoch Beat and three pools. That's up four miles. That's the best, the only good one around here."

Two dismayed fishermen

So much for Hotel literature.

We headed for Perthshire. I had a patient with an estate there so we drove North for advice. The neighbouring Hotel had fishing, all booked, but we took rooms.

"Now Reg" says I "We are going to get fish and that's all there is about it."

On to the telephone and, yes, there was a motor launch and a ghillie available on the South side of Loch Tay half way along, at Ardeonaig.

It was a red letter day. The ghillie was so pleased he had "real fishers" aboard who didn't want to stop for a break and a picnic several times a day.

The four of us sailed off to one of his favoured spots. "No-oh, they're no' rising here today." says Dougal. So, up anchor and off to his next secret hermitage. Dougal knew the locations of fish hideaways and we moved in a mysterious way around Loch Tay.

It is surrounded by high mountains, heather clad and strewn with rock faces and screes. We had all four seasons that day. Beautiful blue skies, warm mellow spring showers, an August breeze and a full blast fall of snow. What more could you ask?

Fishing is not a slow business with a ghillie who is keen for you to have fish. There was a look in Dougal's eye which indicated "attack" – Loch Tay is very large.

Be sure you have the right gear. The layer system of clothing. See that the feet are warm. Have lots of layers of Cashmere pullovers with and without long sleeves. And something like a 'Bell tent' as a waterproof to slip over everything when it snows. And you are in for a treat.

The skies change endlessly. A day which starts 'all blue' can be stormy by eleven o'clock.

A day which starts with a layer of half an inch of snow all over, but a light sky, can become a magic picture highlighting all the myriad of browns of the hill sides. The wind can change in minutes, now from the North, now from the West bringing brilliant cloud formations. The sun hidden behind a dense cloud has so often that silver lining around the edge.

Forget your city ways and start afresh. "Over bright, over early", said with the proper accent, means that when the city dweller sees a fine morning and his hope rises, to the highland ghillie it usually means – "If it is too bright early in the day, it will be very wet in no time."

So you are best in the hands of those who know, as I said about post-graduate seminars.

No, we didn't stop for lunch and we had two salmon, *AND* Dougal congratulated us on how we handled the fish!

Reg, my senior, had a twenty pounder. I had a sixteen pounder.

They were photographed and photographed.

DONALD IN SUTHERLAND –
"THE SALMON KNOWS"

T HE East coast of Sutherland has not quite so
many lochs as the West, but the moorlands
and mountains are just as magnificent.

On this occasion we were the guests of the
late H.G. the Duke. His Estate Manager planned every day for us, covering vast areas of the
eastern part of the County. The day usually
began with a drive to a Keeper's cottage,

sometimes almost as remote as just a map reference.

One such day we drove ten miles up a glen on just two metalled tracks to match the wheels of the car. Mile upon mile of moorland, bog, heather, surrounded by hills, high and low. We passed several herds of deer. We put up flocks of partridges and pheasants. The shooting lodge was located at the beginning of a long glen with a splendid loch along the middle.

We were given a boat and fished some bays on both the big loch and a small side one from which ran out a river on its way to the East coast.

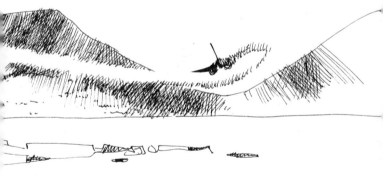

"The salmon knows"

Donald, the Keeper, joined us part of the time and selected a spot of his own on this out-flowing river.

As I do regularly, I gave the rod to him to see 'how it is done'. There is just as much pleasure to be had watching an expert at work as fishing yourself.

The celestial peaceful silence of that glen, with bird calls of grouse, curlew, oyster-catcher, just faintly heard from distant gullies or heather patches, was therapeutic to the mind.

Donald was showing me some points on casting and the use of 'the spare hand' to keep hold of all the spare line he was drawing in as he moved the fly in the water.

Suddenly there was the scream of a jet fighter coming whistling up the glen from the narrow entrance. It felt as if it was not more than 100 feet above our heads. It howled up the long loch and rose fast at the end to clear the shoulder between two mountains.

Well, it was a happy reminder that we have a defence force.

However, something else happened.

A long submarine-like hump in the water moved slowly and precisely up the length of the water we were fishing.

Later, Donald had that salmon and gave me the rod to play the fish, which he gaffed.

The salmon knew that something had been going on above him. One wonders if this now common event in the highlands – low flying fighter aircraft making such a noise – has an effect on the spawning of fish.

And Donald's wife had laid on a splendid Scots tea for us. Everything home-baked.

A SALMON IN A TROUT NET. MY WIFE ON THE DON, ABERDEEN

OUR very first 'unattended by ghillie' salmon we caught on the River Don in Aberdeen-shire. I was fishing for trout. There was a high bank at one pool on the stretch of water. From the top of this bank one could see straight down in to the depths of the slow running water. There before us lay six black submarines – salmon. The nearest lay in a part of the pool near our bank, tucked behind a very large boulder.

I began to spin for this fish. As the line arched its way round at the speed of the current my lure passed high over the fish's head. It had to. It could not 'swim' low enough or it became lodged on this hazard.

We made a plan of attack.

My wife stood high on the bank. As the lure came across the top of the boulder she'd yell "Now!" I'd quickly let out a handful of line and the slack allowed the lure to drop in the water into the pothole where the fish lay.

We became skilled in our co-ordination. We finally annoyed the fish so much he took the lure. We only had a trout landing net.

What followed was rather like a Bateman Cartoon.

The bank was high enough above the water to make it impossible to 'tail the fish'. We tried swimming it into our small trout landing net, which is impossible. When we did land it, we both fell upon it with a shout, dismissed its life

A salmon in a trout net

very speedily and rushed up over the bank to lock it in the boot of the car.

The local village butcher obliged by keeping the fish in his fridge until we could organise transport to Aberdeen for smoking.

The salmon eventually arrived in London and we spent a happy evening doing an almost ceremonial carving of our catch. The slices were packed in quantities for two and four helpings and placed in the freezer. They kept us and our friends happy for a very long time.

We had been staying in a little pub located in a small community. I asked where the nearest Post Office was located, I needed a stamp. The proprietor took me into his dining room and opened a Victorian sideboard cupboard and fetched out a standard-sized cigar box. That was the Post Office.

CALLED BEFORE
HEADMASTER HAMISH IN
WESTER ROSS

I HAVE never been dressed down in less uncertain terms. I felt like a novice, well, that was what I was, as far as Hamish was concerned.

There are lots of sparkling trout rivers north of Ullapool. And we had permission to fish a long stretch of one which had good pools at points where the river had sharp bends. We were a family party of seven and made our base camp off the small second class approach road. Off we went to our mile of river bank. Some were learning and they stuck together. Others wandered off over the horizon.

It was a mixture of broken-up stream I was fishing. My line was going out well beyond a large fallen tree to deep water. Well, it was a tempting place in spite of the hazard of this immense obstacle right in front of me. But then, I was carried away by the sense of being out in the fresh air and by the various sights and sounds of a highland scene. Discretion and valour receded in the mind because there in front of me was what looked like a piece of deep water with faster flowing edges. Never mind that tree!

I waded out about one third of the way across. Any further and I would be in rather deep water. I had not yet graduated to a wading staff, like serious salmon fishers.

My rod was delivering the cast happily at the edge of the fast flow of water just as it became a side eddy. I was missing the fallen tree. There should be trout just there.

Suddenly something very heavy was on my line. The rod bent very sharply. No, it wasn't a branch of that log. It was moving. That was no trout. It must be a salmon.

Well, that fish changed my entire approach to all my past experience of fishing. Could my rod take it? How about a landing net or gaff? No help from my friends, they were a long way off. I was in pretty deep water. No bank nearby to retreat to. And that big fallen tree.

By the time I had worked out how to get that 'ton-weight' past the fallen tree I was exhausted. I got the fish to my waders three times. My trout net was of no use. I was then too tired to try tailing the fish. I did try. He was well enough hooked to have been landed by the usual methods but not for my escapade and he found a moment when I was unable to hold the line tight and he was off. I lost him.

All that was bad enough. But of course I had to tell my story to the ghillie Hamish, who was out with the rest of the party.

Headmaster Hamish asks why

WHOSE FISH ARE THEY ON THE ESTUARY OF THE YTHAN?

THE river Ythan (Ithan to the Southerner), rises at Ythan Wells many miles inland near the town of Huntly, at the heart of agricultural Aberdeenshire. That end has always been known to my family. My parents were born, brought up and farmed beside its source. The graveyard of the little church carries the evidence.

The modern factories further toward the sea have not helped with the pollution of the water, but it is still a sea-trout river.

The estuary is a fascinating place. It does not run in at right angles to the coast, but runs North as well as West, so there is a long

fingerlike peninsula of sandy bank on the North side of the estuary.

This is the nesting place for the Tern.

The tern is a graceful, slender bird, less marine and more specialised than the gull. It has a pointed dagger-like bill and a forked tail. Sea terns are white with black caps and feed by diving into the water.

This local possessor of the land, or rather of the snout of the sandy peninsula is a fellow fisherman,. He is a good guide to the presence of fish.

The whole of this scene centres around the ghillie, Peter. He has put in many years on the Estuary. He sits there quietly in charge, but you sense his wisdom and experience as the tide moves in, the weather changes and the strong wind calls for his skill in handling the boat.

What makes ghillies, ghillies, then becomes real as he responds to the kaleidoscopic ever changing conditions and peace prevails. Yet

"The tern and I went for the same sea trout"

91

another lesson for the fast streams of modern life.

As I sat there in the boat it was obvious that Peter and the tern knew what was going on down below. We were together, just two boat lengths apart – a cluster of six terns hovering within range of my cast and just three feet above the water. One could watch in close-up their diving procedure.

It was inevitable then, that at some point we would both go for the same fish, and it happened. My lure was obviously right over the fish and the tern took it. The terns seem to survive these mishaps of joint assault.

It is probably the only time I'll ever have a tern in my hand, to have a look at this finely proportioned bird. It seemed none the worse when released. "One good tern deserves another."

I suppose it matters if one concentrates on 'success stories', to know every productive lie of fish running up the estuary, all the way from the sea, and to know the state of the tide to suit each. Success stories are not the ones about the size of the catch, but about the effect that the signs of nature have on your thinking; the rise and fall of the tide; the weed which has appeared from nowhere. You have experienced the effect of the brackish water – fresh coming down the river – salt coming in with the tide.

And that constant sandy suspension in the tidal water which penetrates every strand of the line on the reel and results in much time cleaning when you are not out on the Estuary.

This attitude to fishing puts the days of 'no fish' into perspective. And if you do not have that, you have yet to understand the message.

Jim Last.

JIM LAST ON SCONE
PALACE WATER, THE
TAY

STRESS is not confined to the Board Room or
Work Bench. Both ghillie and physician see
it as a part of their daily round of work.

Stress in the salmon under the water and
stress in the angler on the bank shifts the whole
responsibility for understanding and cure to the
ghillie. Both jobs are "a labour of love" says Jim
Last, who cares for the Scone Palace water
above Perth. The tide almost reaches that
water, so all the story of salmon river fishing
begins there.

There is not a day in the year he is not on that
stretch of water. And that has been going on for
the last nine years. He has been in the profession of ghillie for seventeen years. His is the
24–hour day. One of his sons has already
decided to follow father's footsteps.

Like the physician dealing with stress, Jim
knows his guests. As he says: "Some come to
fish to get away from the telephone." "Some just
enjoy fishing. They tie their own flies." "Some
pay a lot of money to fish (fish against the clock)
and they want fish. They are called 'fishmon-
gers'."

"When the water is low in the river" says Jim,
"the fish may stay in a pool for anything up to
six weeks. The signs of stress are the spots of
fungus which begin to show on the top of the
head. It is one thing to feel happy that the guest
is getting fish, but the feeling for these anxious
marooned fish, unable to move up river, is very
present in my mind."

Jim Last has the continuous care of three miles of bank. Cutting the grass and weed to a width of 15 feet can take 6 weeks early in the year. It was heavy going when it all had to be done by hand scythe. Fortunately the modern whizzing nylon spinning thread (weed-eater) relieves the effort somewhat.

Jim's first fishing rod was acquired when he was 8 years old. It was the shaft of a golf club, with a picture ring attached at the top. It had a light line of string and a hook for a worm at the end. So he was set for his first success on the river Almond nearby his present stretch on the Tay and no distance from where he was born in Scone village. His next treasure was a Hardy's green heart rod bought for him by his uncle.

A lifetime of fishing produces important observations. Fish are passing up river in two long periods. The Spring run on the Tay is from January to May. The autumn run is from July to October. Their spawning time is always the autumn no matter when they enter the river. By then they are up into the rivers Dochart, Lyon, Tummell and Garry. The deeper parts of Loch Tay must have a lot of fish through the summer as they await the autumn run up the rivers.

So what's the difference between a trout fly and a salmon fly?

I had watched Bill on the river Test change my fly every fifteen minutes in the gathering darkness of the evening rise, when we did not seem to be matching the fly which was hatching on the water.

But the salmon fly? And what puts the salmon into the mood to take it?

Says Jim: "If they are not in the mood, they will take nothing."

So, what puts them into the mood?

"Salmon are predatory fish and will snap at anything. The pattern is NOT important on the Tay. It is the size that matters. And they appear to respond to the state of the weather, the temperature and the light."

Yes, I recalled the occasion on the Dee in Aberdeenshire when with my wife's co-operation we crossed the nose of a salmon so many times it got cross and took our spinner.

The story of the river is changing all the time. Early in the summer the three year old fish will be coming up river. This maiden fish or grilse has passed through the stages since spawning as alevin, fry, parr, smolt and set out for the sea after two years in the river. Now it has returned to the river after one year at sea. They weigh 3 lb; 6 lb; by late August 8 lb in weight. The fish has probably spent a year around Greenland. It is fascinating why the five year old fish chooses to stay at sea for three years, not one. This fish can be 18 lb and upwards.

Sadly too, 90% will die after spawning. They are to be found by the bank, these kelts. They rarely survive. If they do get to the sea they cannot defend themselves and become food for larger deep sea fish and seals.

Jim has a constant record of nature's story. Winter time can be as rewarding even if fishing is not on. He can watch fish leap in the water during spawning. He is biologist, ornithologist, water gardener. May and June not only necessitates bank cutting but weed cutting in the water. When the water is low and a lot of nitrates have been sprayed on the adjacent fields, evidence is there at the mouths of the burns which flow into the Tay. There is a fast growth of crowfoot weed in the river with its great pillows of small white flowers. When the water is even lower, great sheets of blanket weed have to be dealt with.

And there are some trout in these peaceful pools formed by the piers, jetties, croys, beside the hut at Waulkmill.

But there are predators to be dealt with as well. In the middle of the night, small inflatable dinghies with a net between can be silently moved on to the water. They can make a sweep in the darkness netting salmon. The design of these fraudulent nets makes it possible for the salmon to swim through one outer, wide mesh net to a second layer with a finer mesh. The fish is caught by its gills and it cannot reverse backwards. To deal with these maurauders' nets it has become necessary to sink concrete slabs with a metal triple hook to snare the thieves'.

But Jim Last shows his complete oneness with the river as he describes the pleasure watching someone playing a fish. He is playing the fish with them.

That August afternoon (1987) I had a seven pound salmon from the Lower Scone Beat. The fish was fresh run from the sea with lice on its head and three years old.

Next day Iain and I had three more Salmon.

FISHING IN TOTAL DARKNESS WITH BOB IN DEVON

I T was after dinner at our little Hotel on Dartmoor and dusk was approaching.

"Would you like to try fishing at night?" said the Water Bailiff, in the lounge.

It had been a glorious day. We walked to a stream, well, a brook, and the sun had shone and fishing was forgotten, as my wife and I had a picnic on that wide open undulating moorland. We were saturated in fresh air and ready for bed.

But an invitation from the Bailiff was a treat hardly to be expected and not to be refused. It did not take long to make a decision. My wife went off to bed. He couldn't look after two in the dark.

An hour later, about eleven p.m., the Bailiff and I set off to his chosen stream. By the roadside we put up our two fly-rods and his special selection of flies. It was a still night, very dark, no moon. Cool but not cold. Owls hooted from several directions. My reflexes were somewhat on edge as I had no idea what was going to happen. And just suppose I got my cast and line in a tangle? How was I to deal with that in the dark? Could I rise to the challenge and not disappoint the bailiff?

I was allowed a small hand torch. But then, I only had two hands. Although a landing net could be clipped on to my belt, I still had to take hold of the bailiff's coat and carry my rod. And the path was soon one of those super highways, worn into shape by sheep – well, they may think they are highways. They are firm enough, if it hasn't rained recently and if you can see just where you are putting your feet. And that is never at regular intervals. Sometimes they are narrow, sometimes they disappear under a tuft of heather or moorland grass which has fallen over. Sometimes there is a pothole filled with water, not a path at all. The highway never goes in the same direction for more than two paces, so you miss it more often than you hit it. And there is the rod to be cared for. Never been an issue in my life before, these sheep trails! So, the bailiff's coat tail becomes a third leg if you see what I mean.

Bad enough getting over fences in the daytime. Sometimes the line or cast gets a little loose from its prepared 'travelling position' against the rod. In the daylight this can be captured before disaster overtakes.

Soon I was cautioned to proceed slowly.

"We're nearly there" said the bailiff quietly.

I could not see a thing.

"Just forward a little" – he taking my shoulders and rotating me a little clockwise.

"There you are" he whispered. "Right on the edge of the pool."

I still could not see a thing.

Well, perhaps the top half of my line of vision was a shade lighter than the bottom half, if I looked very critically.

"Just stand right there and cast directly in front of you" he whispered. "I'll go down the bank a bit and if you raise a fish give me a shout."

Phew, I was all alone. No idea what was in front of me but just instructions to get on with it, my reputation at stake.

"Watch how you cast" I said to myself. "It

would be rather immature to get the line and flies tangled. I'm supposed to be a fly-fisher."

Out flew the line into nowhere.

"Yes, I think that landed without too much of splash."

"No, I didn't tangle the line." "Perhaps a little further this time?"

My guide had really disappeared and I could see absolutely nothing. Didn't know if I could step to right or left or back. Certainly not forward . . .

Try and try again.

"Good heavens, I have a trout!" The rod point went down fast. I could feel it as the line screamed off the reel. Fortunately the fish had hooked itself well. I gave a shout and the bailiff responded somewhere off to my left in the darkness.

Of course my pride at having a fish 'on' immediately suggested I have it on the bank before he got back to me.

And I did it. Luck! Thrilling experience.

It was acknowledged over breakfast next morning.

The experts will show us their graphs which will prove that as the moon progresses in the production of light or at the break of day, the trout are in a hurry for a quick meal, and so forth.

It all reminded me of Campbell, up in Sutherland: "He'll no' rise unless he gets everything his own way."

4
Guardians of a Heritage

SAMPLING THE HERITAGE, MICK
LUNN, THE HOUGHTON CLUB

FREDERIC M.HALFORD

JIM HADDRELL AT KIMBRIDGE ON
THE RIVER TEST

BILL LOADER AND HIS FRIENDS
ON THE ITCHEN

SAMPLING THE HERITAGE, MICK LUNN, THE HOUGHTON CLUB

THE magic of fly fishing is revealed when Mick Lunn tells of some of the heritage of chalk stream fishing. He will produce the butt end of an eighteen foot bamboo pole rod from the days of blow line fishing. Blow line indeed it was. Attached would be a light floss silk line with a hook on the end with a grasshopper or daddylonglegs. The bamboo pole would be held high straight above the head and the breeze would carry the silk thread and 'lure' out across the water, to be lowered with care at the appropriate spot.

The early spring fishing was a brief six weeks. Grannom fishing in late April and early May, followed by the May fly, and that was the end of the fishing season.

These methods were IN, in the days of horse travel. As we moved to railway travel and the motor car, fishing ways changed too. The whipping rod came along with the beginning of the artificial fly. The construction of rods has followed at the same pace, cane, steel, glass, carbon, graphite. And the line and reel have changed as precisely, as did the move from gut to nylon.

But the Lunn contribution to fly-fishing had more to it than following these changes in the development of an industrial nation. Mick's father began trout farming forty years ago, in 1947 about the time Mick was released from the army. The Lunns led the way for today's farming of trout and salmon. Father made what today would be described as original research, the use of spring water for the rearing of trout.

Their spring (bore hole) brought up water from deep down. The quality of it was that it was clear of sediment and at a constant temperature 10°C/50°F. The value of this find is important because trout which breed in the river have to survive the byproduct of the peat deposit in the river Test valley – marsh gas, methane. This, mixed into the river water takes a toll of the young alevin trout and kills many of them. In a hatchery supplied with spring water this toll is overcome. What is more, the 80/90 day incubation period of the river is reduced to 42 days in the spring water hatchery.

The hatchery trout, having ideal conditions for growth, can be released into the river at the end of March. They are old enough then to survive the methane impurity.

The river water temperature is also rising by that time to 50°F which matches the water they were bred in from the spring/bore. What is more, the spring water is not polluted by bugs, so the fish are kept healthy during these first important months.

He has moved on from the days when fish food was horse flesh chopped up and finely minced, to today's well balanced pellet feeds.

Mick was old enough in his years before he was 12, to acquire the full flavour of grandfather Lunn's skills before he died. He taught him how to tie a fly. He caught his first trout by his side. He learned to slip into the chicken hut and steal a suitable feather for fly tying with grandfather, whose flies like Lunn's Particular are renowed world wide.

Men like Mick's grandfather and Frederic Halford were entomologists, almost before being fishermen. There has been a Lunn, father and grandfather for over one hundred years on the Houghton Club water on the Test. Grandfather came to Stockbridge in 1886. Lunn and Halford were among the pioneers of today's many applications of fly design.

Grandfather Lunn had had a difficult upbringing; running away from an unkind stepfather, he found work on a farm, then as a keeper's boy. There was a curious interlude when he became a bank messenger at the Union Bank in Princes Street. There he was spotted by Herbert Norman of the great family of bankers and taken down to be his ghillie in 1886. Norman recognised the Lunn gift for wresting the secrets of nature from the countryside and asked him to look after the interests of the Club.

The Houghton Club had been launched in 1822 when two men Edward Barnard and Canon Beadon acquired the lease of water by the village of Houghton (two miles from Stockbridge). They co-opted twelve others to join them and the membership over the years has been allowed to increase to twentyfour. The authority for its world renown lies in intimate matters such as its Records, which have been kept from the very beginning, every fish caught and on which fly and on what Beat of the river, carefully noted.

Mick's father was Head Keeper from 1931. Mick, now just past sixty years of age, left school at sixteen in 1942, was commissioned with the 1st. Battalion, the Devonshire Regiment served in the far East, India, Malaya, Hong Kong until demobilisation in January 1948. He became keeper of the lower Houghton water and in 1963, twentyfour years ago, took over from his father as Head Keeper.

FREDERIC M. HALFORD

" ANGLERS should know that their sport in
the coming season is largely dependent
on the quality and quantity of the work done by
the keeper during the short days of the fall and
winter . . . it is a lonely life on the river bank."

"An honest, sober, hardworking, intelligent
man who starts with the intention of devoting
himself to the fishing . . . he must be paid liberal
wages and have a comfortable cottage near the
stream . . . such a keeper must be treated with
courtesy and consideration."

"The capacity for imparting knowledge to
others is a natural gift like an ear for music or
talent for drawing. A moderate performer who
possesses this capacity is a far better teacher
than the highest exponent of the art who is
without it."

These three quotes come from: *The Dry-Fly
Man's Handbook*, by F. M. Halford. Nearly one
hundred years ago he was saying these things
about water keepers and he inferred that good
keepers were difficult to find.

One cannot go far with serious dry-fly fishing
without coming across his name. Fishermen,
water keepers, ghillies need to be reminded of
their heritage.

Such men develop a magic veneer, an aura.
They deserve this, without losing sight of the
fact that they were ordinary people. Halford
was a sort of apostle, ancestor to dry-fly fishers.

There were lots of others who fished, but the
fascination of the life of the trout on the river
Test turned him into an entomologist primarily,
rather than a fisherman. Halford's love of

104

entomology, reflecting normal talk with today's ghillie, was very strong.

He began with the photography of flies and became interested in creating floating flies. Halford was different from the rest, because he was the one who wrote down the story of the river fly. He chronicled everything; from the content of fish stomach after anatomical dissection which disclosed the flies of choice, to the contemplation of what creates for the fish, a happy time for life. He recorded their sex and weight.

His first analysis was directed to what they ate at the top of the water, not down at the bottom. Soon this was related to the conditions of the weather, when he got no fish. Lack of a 'basket' was not a disappointment to him – just part of the study of fish life. His Diaries recorded every day of each season, fish caught or not caught. The now brown with age photographs in the Halford Collection, enhance the research task he had undertaken.

The breadth and detail of Halford's thinking on dry fly fishing are evidenced in these further quotes from the Handbook:

"The stronger the adverse wind the more rapidly the beginner casts and the more strength he puts into it. He should do exactly the reverse – the stronger the wind the slower should be the motion, and when once he has succeeded in getting the pace of the rod, he will find the force required is very little more against a violent wind than against a light one.

"Purists, those of us who will not under any circumstances cast except over rising fish are sometimes called ultra-purists, and those who will occasionally try to tempt a fish in position, but not actually rising are styled purists . . . Marryat used to say that a day at the riverside watching a first-rate performer was quite as enjoyable as one passed in solitude fishing oneself . . . when our long-expected guest arrives it is perhaps during a spell of unpropitious weather . . . the pastmaster will in such case possess his soul in patience . . . It is the very worst of taste for a guest to flog it down with a wet fly, because he should know it is the unwritten law of the dry fly man on a chalk stream to eschew any but the legitimate method . . . his hospitable friend will abstain from making any remark on the subject, although his unspoken thoughts may be most eloquent."

"The great secret of rising a trout with the dry fly is to combine accuracy and delicacy at the first cast."

"I had Hardy's make me the 9ft. 6in. rod, weighing 8oz. 14dr., on the model of the 'Halford' 1905 rod . . this latter weighed 11½oz., so the reduction of weight is considerable." (My Orvis 'Advantage' rod, 9ft. 3ins., is 3⅛oz.)

The portrait of Frederic Halford, in the home of his great-grandson John, shows a distinguished looking man, about 5ft. 10in. high. He was a very kind person and loved children. He was 70 when he died. Born in 1844, he died in 1914. Halford ceased his business interests at the age of 45 and set out to discover "What makes fishing work?" That was about 100 years ago. Halford and the river Test are almost synonymous. His fishing books for the dry fly man are as much to the point as any modern 'How to do it' book.

His son Ernest was not 'a fisherman', but Ernest's son Cecil, certainly was. He loved fishing right from boyhood. Grandfather taught him. He could not resist using grandfather's rods and tackle. He was not to know these would become treasures. Great-grandson John says of the collection of memorabilia: "How to give the world pleasure from the past?" In time all the Halford records will be on show. Like great-grandfather Frederic and father Cecil, John has natural wisdom of the countryside. He breeds racehorses with that special care needed for mares as they foal, followed by the crucial period prior to their start of racehorse training. He also breeds that beautiful bird, the Macaw.

My first dry fly trout

When the direct descendants of Frederic are your first patients, and you look after the family for nearly forty years, 'fishing' is likely to come up in the conversation. It is not surprising that on the occasion of celebrating forty years in professional life with a dinner for loyal patients who have become friends, the Halfords should turn out in force and claim their rightful place on my right and bring a unique present – a splendid gift indeed. A May fly tied by the great man himself. It is a treasure now in possession of my nephew Iain who has done the drawings for this book. The Halfords told me I was the only person to have been given one – "Not even the family has one." That was in March 1973.

MAY FLY – Frederic M. Halford

107

My good fortune continued. Ten years later I attended a Sale of fishing and shooting 'Items' by Sotheby's at Gleneagles Hotel in August 1982. Listed in the Catalogue I spotted: "Halford, F. M., *The Dry-Fly Man's Handbook*; illustrated, original cloth, octavo, 1913" Well, I just had to have that book.

I was present because I had decided to sell a Salmon Fly Rod, with spliced joints, 13ft., with spare tip, metal carrying case (all in great detail in the Catalogue). It fetched £90 and by the time the auctioneer had his commission I got enough to have the Halford book for £65. BUT, the Halford book was Item 104 and the Rod was Item 195, so I had to bid for the book before I knew how much I would get for the rod. More excitement, but worth it.

The Halfords kept inviting me and my wife to stay with them by the Test and fish their rod at Leckford. I really feared to go as I was a highland-ghillie-trained-apprentice-wet-fly fisher. In the end I said: "All right, I'll come if you will teach me to fish the dry fly."

"The pellucid clearness of the water" Cecil Halford called it and I was sitting beside it.

Of course, my thought was to get going. But no, said the ghillie: "We'll just sit here for a little." My next experience of water-keepers began as he talked about the countryside. It was the time when the evening rise was due. This meant nothing to me. Then sure enough, one fly, then two or three appeared on the water and took off from their 'aircraft carrier'. To my amazement there appeared 'the magic circle' – a trout rising to feed.

This fish was not moving around. It always rose at the same spot. You could tell as the next fly came across his path that he would come up. Then there were two, then three precise spots where trout rising rings appeared on the water, precisely placed. Soon the water-keeper was telling me the size of each trout by the size of the marking on the water. Marks were appearing all the way down the stretch of river we could see. Then he suggested which ones we should go for.

My apprenticeship in dry-fly fishing had begun. Fortunately on my first evening a gentle breeze got up with a resulting ripple on the water. So my casting did not have to be quite so skilled to deceive the fish. Test trout are well educated.

I now have two trout from the Test in a bow-fronted glass case on my wall: "My first trout caught with the dry-fly. 1lb. 4oz. & 1lb: Beat II Leckford, May 2nd. 1954."

(Leckforde was indeed "a parifh and place of cure" as described on John Norden's map of HAMSHIRE engraved by William Hole for Camden's "Britannia" 1610).

JIM HADDRELL AT KIMBRIDGE ON THE RIVER TEST

HE was in the Gurkha Rifles and on Landing Craft in World War II, and he is in the mould of Frederic Halford. He has been on the Test for fifteen years.

Jim Haddrell's philosophy is summed up – pointing to his heart – "If you're not happy here, you won't be happy anywhere."

Well, just suppose he said to you: "The Vikings used to put their deceased Chieftain in a boat, set it alight and push it out to sea. That was burial. I think you should use your old rod as kindling for the fire, as they did." It was a splendid start for our fishing encounter. It was how he described my life-treasured split-cane rod, when I demonstrated my technique.

He relented: "Perhaps you should hang it on your wall to recall happy memories." I sent it to the vast Spring Sale of fishing tackle, soon to take place nearby.

In the mould of Halford he continued: "Casting has nothing to do with physical effort in the forearm. You need to discover 'the Aristocratic Stoop'. Casting is done from the waist, NOT from the eight muscles which form the flexing compartment of the forearm." Well, they were nearly his words. Power is there because the weight of the line is balanced to the spring recoil in the graphite rod. That is what carries the cast to its destination. No more fighting against the wind. Halford was saying that nearly a hundred years ago.

"The aristocratic stoop"

Yes, Jim's muscles are firm, but the scene reminded me of another river Test master, the late Sir Ivan Magill – 50 years a member of the Houghton Club. He was like an uncle to me. He would display his splendid right arm muscles, developed from expert fly casting over the years. This would happen at the end of operating sessions in the London Clinic when he had given anaesthetics for my patients. "Maggi" to the exclusive Houghton Club, "The Boss" to me, was the world doyen of anaesthesia. "Plastic surgery was founded on the work of Magill." said Sir Harold Gillies.

When fishing a long line (and Jim is always telling you to keep the tip of the rod at water level), how do you get it in the air to change direction, so that you can place the fly on a different spot on the water? Never snatch it off the water. It makes a mess of the surface. Pull a little in gently, so that it is not too long. Then lift the point of the rod very slowly accelerating to the 10.30 position (the Aristocratic Stoop), before smartly delivering it in the air from 10.30 to 12.00 (hand on rod in front of the right eye) in a high back cast.

As this final upward impulse is made, pull in a yard of line with the left hand in co-ordination, *equally sharply*.

Says Jim: "60% of people have paralysed left hands and can't do it. 30% do it in such a genteel fashion, it doesn't work."

Kimbridge on the Test, with ORVIS

Suddenly in the midst of concentration on spotting the location of trout taking occasional flies he'll say: "There's a fine water vole under that bank over there, rootling around."

Sound ideas on trout fishing pop out all the time: "Never pull the knot tight with dry nylon. Always wet it or the heat of the friction will weaken the nylon."

When my nephew had a one and a quarter pound grayling, (after he had had a two and a quarter pound rainbow trout), Jim fetched his knife and began de-scaling it immediately: "If you don't do it now, it will be all over the kitchen – and you know what that means."

Jim is the Orvis Company's Master Teacher and a day out with him on the Test is an encapsulated version of country life from every aspect; the knowledge of a man of the river, like Halford; the patience of a teacher who is successful because he pulls no punches on your performance – as a Royal gentleman found out.

Halford and Haddrell were for effortless fishing. And tradition and logic were well matched. "No fighting against the wind" said Halford and Jim demonstrated the aristocratic stoop to fulfil the old master's craft.

There is nothing dull about a day with Jim at Kimbridge, from the first and immediate cup of coffee by the river. As a writer on the philosophy of Clinical Practice, with the subject of Stress at its core, tradition and logic had to be examined by me. I usually held the rod with the right hand. When I set a hook in a fish I rapidly switched hands, to wind the reel with the right hand. But those first few split seconds are vital in the contact with a rising trout.

Jim was aware of my new proposition of keeping the rod in my right hand and attending to my 'tight line' with my left. He just smiled at my academic mind at work on tradition and logic. It was Richard Banbury in the Orvis Shop, a casting pundit, whose logic convinced me to move my right hand winding reel to left hand winding.

On the Test that day it was obvious that I could forget all the spare line at my feet and pay attention to the bend at the top of the rod, which told me if my hair thin leader could take that amount of strain. Logic overtook tradition.

Nether Wallop Mill

The sense of touch has always been central to good surgery and to supreme dry-fly fishing. The fine embroideries in the John Russell home (He is Managing Director at Orvis) indicate his fine touch with the trout rod. (Half the embroideries are his work. The other half have been done by his wife.)

But if you enter Jim's world I suggest you get your lady to find you a 12 inch strip of webbing, about 2 inches wide, with Velcro on it. I call it the Haddrell Training Wrist Strap. Get some-one to wind it around your wrist AND rod, quite firmly and you will find you're well on the way to performing the aristocratic stoop correctly, with the rod moving up to the right eye, and no further.

He says you can go on fishing in the old way with your split-cane rod, just as you may drive your 1930 Bentley (I used to have one) and enjoy it, but modern dry-fly fishing with the 'Catch and release' system gives refreshment to so many more of us.

There is a spot on the Orvis Kimbridge Beat, where you can wade out to an island and fish two pieces of fast water, just like up North.

And with my 'Advantage' rod/line balance, there is no problem about landing the fly on the water under the branches of an overhanging tree. It's a new day. It can take a long time for the Halford truths to surface.

BILL LOADER ON THE ITCHEN AND HIS FRIENDS
Guardians of the pristine clear water of the Test and Itchen, Hampshire

FEBRUARY is a good month to have an unhurried dinner party with ghillies.

Winter is losing some of its sharpness. Colour has come suddenly to the drab winter scene with large patches of yellow aconites, followed by splashes of white snowdrops in sheltered places.

The men of the country are turning their mind to the repairs needed by the river banks. They have finished their spell of support for the grouse shooters, loading their guns, walking up the birds. Water keeping needs their full attention.

Biotechnology is coming to the rescue of these underwater gardeners and entomologists. It is heartening to know, as the Director of the Biotechnology Department of the University of Cambridge forecasts, that with the fast advance in cell nucleus engineering, a new corn seed will be produced, which when drilled will have in its structure the necessary elements for growth, which will eliminate the spraying of crops and the pollution of the rivers.

I had recently spent time with Bill Loader on the Itchen and he had invited his friends Pat Fox and Ray Hill to join us.

We spent three hours around the dinner table at the Carbery Guest House, Stockbridge, eating a good meal, the four of us reflecting on the lessons of the past year. My three guests were experienced river keepers. All were aware of the fast changing scene in the country.

We were talking about the philosophy of life which attracts six million from every walk of life, to fishing.

Pat, water keeper and ghillie for twenty years on the Itchen, and ten years before that on the Kennett, had the view that almost 50% just fish to experience the solitude. Does that suggest anything? "Something went out of life with the arrival of the Idiot's Lantern – the T.V. box." He was appraising the value of the ghillie's job of setting the scene for such contemplation, but added: "You can't stop progress, but it was more fun fifty years ago. Nowadays the equipment doesn't perish. We used to spend hours looking after it. Cat gut was more readily broken. Line had to be dried."

Solitude and contemplation were central to Pat's mind. He described an elderly professional man who came one morning to fish the Itchen. He put up his rod and went to sit by the river. Lunch time came. He returned to the hut to eat his sandwiches and back he went to his chosen spot, with his rod. In the evening he returned to the hut, took his rod down. He had not fished all day, nor had he said a word. As he left he said: "We'll sort them out tomorrow'."

These water keepers have set a pattern for the friendship of the river bank. Pat recalled: "My salary forty years ago was three pounds, four shillings and six pence per week. At that time I was looking up some early records of wages. A water keeper got two shillings and six pence per week. But one such record of payment by the Head Keeper noted that one keeper got two shillings and nine pence – three pence more. "COS 'E GOT 8 KIDS."

The Itchen in early spring

The ghillie has a calling as well defined as that of any specialist we may turn to when sick. It is the treasure in the man. The fisherman may not take the time to read his ghillie. There is no doubt the ghillie will read him.

It is a long and varied road to become a good ghillie. As with the healing professions, people come first and techniques second. Of course our skills give us authority, but that has to be taken as basic to success. Pat summed up: "When a ghillie is young or starting out, he assumes that he is meeting people who are senior to him in age, have money and may be in the twilight of their years. Knowing that the person is likely to be quite clever, the ghillie will not be given to saying too much. When he does make a pronouncement, it is likely to have a lot of foundation to it."

Ray Hill, (a third generation keeper) on the Test with the Houghton Club, put it clearly: "One appreciates the life we live by the river when we have to go to London. We are much more philosophical, because we know we can't shift things we see going on in nature." He recalled the deep impression some birds can have on you. "On a still night, the song of the nightingale will float up the valley. It is very impressive. The atmosphere impregnates people."

This awareness of nature produces a new level of understanding in other ways. Trustworthiness in reading human nature has been built-in for generations, although these men rarely talk about it. Their examples were moving. The tools they use for their underwater gardening have been the same for generations as well. Pat chipped in: "The tools like the hand scythe and the chain scythe have not changed since the 17th. century."

He recalled what tradition does for people. He was walking up the Itchen with a well-known professor who suddenly said: "Just think of the great men who have walked up this bank before me!"

Bill enlarged on the Spring preparations of the river, such as the March exercise to rid the trout water of the pike, that crafty fish which could burrow down in the mud, change colour, become invisible, making removal extremely difficult.

Spring in the air reminded him of a bird which had come to stay and breed. The female was sitting on her nest on an island. She was disturbed by Bill's presence and called to her cock bird husband. The male flew in on the attack and landed on Bill's back. This largest goose – 95cm, the Canada Goose, with its noisy trumpet-like honking is heavy when it hits you on the back, says Bill. "We have a flock of fifty and they have begun to breed."

I asked about the fast change which takes place in June and Pat commented: "The Ranunculus can grow 12 inches in 24 hours. The pull of water encourages this fast stretching process." It was clear that weed cutting was a matter for much wisdom. Fish need food from the great pillows of green and brown weed, specially toward the end of the season when spawning approaches.

Next morning I visited the Loaders at their thatched cottage for a cup of coffee, and Bill presented me with two pigeons he had shot with the air rifle he had on loan from Pat. "You have to shoot them through the head." says Bill, demonstrating the telescopic sight and silencer.

Back home my wife got busy plucking the birds. She did a splendid piece of surgery. The two pigeons produced four breasts, eight ounces in weight.

These she fried in butter, approximately five minutes each side. They were removed from the pan with the juice.

One onion was chopped and softened in butter in the pan.

The breasts were chopped and put back in the pan briefly. Some herbs, parsley, black pepper, salt were added.

All transferred to a blender and very well mixed.

Two ounces of melted butter and a dessertspoonful of brandy were poured into the mixture.

Blended briefly.

Put into a terrine with a dessertspoonful of melted butter poured over the top and thus into a refrigerator.

This is *Pigeon Paté*, invented by my wife.

Bill's bees produced special honey too.

5

How Others Fish

MY GUV'NOR TEACHES ME TO FISH
OFF CORNWALL WITH FRED

NOTHING LESS THAN THREE POUNDS
WITH BRUCE IN NEW ZEALAND

WITH HANK OFF FLORIDA

"A SHARK!" "A SHARK!"

YES, IT CAN GO TO YOUR HEAD

YOUR VERY OWN WATER

MY GUV'NOR TEACHES ME
TO FISH OFF CORNWALL
WITH FRED

IT'S an all round job being a senior partner in practice. My guv'nor was the perfect example of how to develop a junior associate. He took me sea fishing off Cornwall, a good thing for a trout fisher to do.

In his customary way everything had been laid on. The Hotel was right by the water's edge on the Estuary. Our ghillie, Fred, appeared at the Hotel jetty at the right time. He brought his twentyfour foot motor boat alongside, tackle ready, and off we went in search of Bass.

We sailed out of the estuary and away towards a series of headlands. The weather was fine and warm and there was only a faint ripple on the Atlantic ocean. Each wave of the swell, from the tip of one to the tip of the next, must have been 20 yards. It was hardly perceptible.

There were a few birds around. Besides gulls, both mature white ones and young grey ones, there were cormorants. These black birds with long thin neck and head, and wings set almost at the tail, give the impression of being powerful as they sweep across the surface of the sea, just two feet off the water, in pairs.

A steady breeze to break the surface, a spot of heat and sunshine to produce a hatch of flies and you are on the way to taking trout from a highland loch. That was the list in my mind of fishing requirements. But this was sea-fishing and there appeared to be a longer list; spring and neap tides, ebb and flow, estuary and feeding grounds, rocks and headlands, the depth at which you fish.

Fred had caught the bait that morning before 7 a.m. His box of bait was of special design, about fourteen inches long, shaped like a metronome case, full of sand eels. There were all sizes from 1½ inches to 7 inches in length. The box sides were perforated. It hung over the side of the boat in the water at the fishing grounds, so the eels stayed alive all day. Most of them did. This bait is not damaged greatly by the hook, which is passed through the floor of the mouth and then through the muscle by the lower border of the body, just back of the head. It swims naturally when dropped into the water.

I did not know what to expect. The 8 foot sea fishing rod felt very stiff, compared to my trout rods. It didn't give me the impression that the tip could bend when a fish was 'on'. The cast was six feet in length and had a small metal, free-swivel lure on the end AND the eel.

A light lead weight was placed on the line about two feet up from the join of the cast. The weight of lead depends on how far down you want to fish, always bearing in mind that the cast, with its lure will float upwards from that lead weight.

I didn't realise that the tide was running so fast that it took time for the lead weight to get down through the water.

Came the first excitement. Fred was an expert ghillie and an experienced boatman. He could keep the engine and propeller screws turning in such a way that the line would immediately move off as in a stream, the boat held stationary just a few yards off some great rugged rocks over which the Atlantic seas would be churning and rushing by the cliff face. As the long slow swell moved up the channels we would rise ten or fourteen feet. This is a brand of seamanship fascinating to watch amidst the concentrations on fishing. It is a fine art.

I was soon to learn that there are certain rules you must never forget. I nearly lost my first bass because I was taken by surprise.

We had just got going under our second headland when I struck a fish. Fred will say what fish you've got by the first few tugs on your line. My first reaction, as a trout man, was to let the fish dive, take line and then get tension on it and keep the rod point 'tension-curve' present,. It is the rod point that 'kills the fish', by tiring it. I let the bass have line, then many things went through my mind. The fish feels very heavy. It is going to fight. Is he well hooked? How much can the cast take? Is this type of tug the kind which means I ought to give more line? How much bend should I allow on this firm shafted rod? Could I do some braking of the reel by holding the palm of my hand against it?

It took some moments to sort out these possibilities. Meantime the fish was in control, not me and the line went slack.

I furiously wound my reel and felt a wave of satisfaction as I realised that the fish was 'still there'. The next thing I knew was that there were a series of clearly defined and sharp tugs.

Fred shouted: "That's a bass!" I felt very thrilled as we hadn't had a nibble for two hours. For the first two or three minutes I was confused about what to do. The bass would tug and run. I found myself tucking the big rubber butt of the rod into my tummy. There was

124

enough weight on the fish to give my left hand plenty to do gripping the rod tightly. It became necessary to use the right hand entirely for line control. By placing the palm underneath the reel I could easily adjust the speed at which the bass took line out. I have no idea how many times he went off at speed.

It seemed that there were three phases of fight, all of varying length of time and there was never any warning when one would begin or end.

For long periods the fish would be very tight on the line, but could be wound in. He was probably lying twisted crosswise, so that his 'dead-weight' was what you were pulling. He was not fighting but the tension was great. Then when he had 'taken breath', he'd make off again. That necessitated giving him line, and braking the spin of the reel with the palm of the hand. The very moment he stops fighting to go off, is the time to attempt to bring him nearer.

Once or twice he did the third thing, and I was not ready. He'd swim toward me, slack line, panic stations. Wind in fast to make contact again. After about ten minutes I had him alongside the boat for Fred to net. He was still fighting then and I was jolly tired and quite glad to call it a day. I was surprised to see that he didn't fight after he was brought aboard.

He was 4lb. and a fine silver grey colour.

"Let's get his brother" says I. "Let's get his grandfather" says Fred.

And so to the contemplation of these magnificent Cornish cliffs. The great sea swell. These massive worn-smooth underwater rocks which surface just a few feet away. And Fred in complete charge of a stationary boat amidst a fast running tide, rising and falling in the deep swell of the Atlantic.

A Gannet, cruising around raises the level of contemplation. Flying at 60 feet it suddenly glides, manoeuvres, tips over and goes down in a 60 degree dive hitting the water with almost no splash. Shoal of mackerel down there.

Dreaming, with the clutch off my reel.

Scream of a fish taking – nearly lost the whole line. Fred was not pleased.

The Atlantic swell under the headland

NOTHING LESS THAN
THREE POUNDS, WITH
BRUCE IN NEW ZEALAND

ELEVEN thousand miles is a long way to go to fish. It was not the target of the journey, but the complementary effect of fishing played its usual significant part. I had been working flat out through the illness and death of a younger partner in practice and got exhausted. A long sea voyage was the 'required treatment', no argument! We had a gift of a trip round the world by sea (30,165 miles) on the ships of a grateful patient.

We sailed for New Zealand from Liverpool.

We sailed straight out into a Force 8 gale. We had a broken mooring rope as we turned at the loading quay. The pilot had to be taken to the Isle of Man as the sea was so stormy.

Soon we understood the philosophy of driving a cargo ship. Point it towards the Panama Canal and leave it to get on with it, whatever the weather. After all, a heavy sea won't do any damage to well stowed cargo, which included cargo on the deck.

Out into the Pacific we had our first experience of another marine life, turtles lying flat on the water like great flat ten feet wide discs and flying fish in clouds. We were close to the Galapagos Islands.

If you are a fisherman you cannot stay in New Zealand for a couple of weeks and not fish. Their trout are special. The Motel beside the famous Lake Taupo had a steaming hot swimming pool within the horseshoe of rooms. The geysers of the North Island produce a constant supply of heat, most comforting.

Our New Zealand angling friends laid on the fishing and off we went with permission to enter Lake Rotoaira. We raised no fish.

And the second day we fished and saw no evidence of trout.

The fishing tackle shop owner who supplied the licences to fish, soon got to hear that I was from Scotland and did not appreciate that my collection of New Zealand trophies consisted of a splendid assortment of pumice stones from the shores around the lakes, lovely coloured ones of all sizes – but no fish after two days. His pride was 'on the line'. So he said: "I will come for you at six a.m. tomorrow morning and take you out myself."

I have never seen such dense fog. We got aboard. He looked as though he knew what he was doing, so my fears for our safety were mollified.

We sailed out of his harbour.

I could not see a thing. We were surrounded by white nothingness.

"Well," I thought, "I expect he knows what he is doing." and we sailed on. His conversation about weather conditions – seasonal expectations, the appreciation of trouting habits, filled

Surrounded by white nothingness

in a fresh aspect of the nature of New Zealand. Without that weather I would have missed another glimpse of what makes a good ghillie. But the visibility was still just twenty feet.

I found that the Taupo trout was a 'different kettle of fish'. I could not expect my fly to stay put when he took and I had struck. He has a specially hard mouth and has to be held firmly right into the landing net. No loose landing drill near the boat. We lost one that way. The fish got a fleeting moment when it got under the boat and there was some indecision on our part.

Fish under three pounds in weight are returned to the lake.

Once again it was clear: "Go out with the men who care for the countryside, if you want full refreshment."

The trout we got varied in weight. The best was 21½ inches long and weighed five pounds. It was caught at 6.30 a.m. on May 22nd. 1967.

It was duly laid out on the front page of The New Zealand Herald and its outline drawn in heavy blue pencil. One has to be precise about sizes and weights for future recounting.

A few weeks later we were on the Great Barrier Reef off Queensland, Australia, with its variety of underwater magic.

WITH HANK OFF FLORIDA

FISHING seeps into the thinking quite un-announced. An occasional trip to the country may just be a change from a busy schedule, but each expedition adds something to the ultimate respect for what is available in the therapy of the mind, best achieved through that Consultant, the ghillie.

During a period of a further doctorate in the United States, which occupied every waking moment, my fellow students decided that a Christmas vacation was ahead and something ought to be planned. The program at the University of Pennsylvania was indeed 'the full treatment' with lectures at 8.0 a.m. both winter and summer and laboratory work to do each evening back at the Fraternity House.

A fishing trip to Florida was proposed and four of us set off from the snows of Philadelphia. I had passed my American Automobile Driving test, so could share the driving. It was really a two seater car that Ford, with a 'bulge' or big boot at the back. This opened with the hinge to the rear to uncover 'the rumble seat'. Three sat inside the car and one travelled 'out back' with the luggage, until he froze, then one of the others had to take a turn out in the cold. So, off to the South, a thousand miles away.

Being a 'fast-car' man myself, I got my friends to stop on Daytona Beach for a moment just to let my mind dwell on 'Bluebird' and Sir Malcolm Campbell breaking the world land speed record. So, to the sands of Florida and out in an almost splendid launch to do some deep-sea fishing.

How do we select a ghillie? Which of all these

smart motor launches can we afford? How do we present which lure to the fish? We had a senior academic with us in the party, and he had been here before, so this unlikely fishing party were duly introduced to our ghillie.

Hank was not a big man. He loved his boat, which was not the very latest design, but the metal parts all shone and it had a teak deck for our land-based feet. We quickly appreciated this, because the ship was large enough to cope with all of us forward of his cockpit, as we contemplated sun bathing while awaiting our turn to fish.

Typical of a seasoned ghillie, he showed no sign of the obvious – we knew nothing and he had to start from scratch and tell us what he would be doing and how we should behave when our time came to fish. As men who were accustomed to full concentration on the job, the mix of his full attention to sailing procedure and our willingness to expect anything, it was a memorable scene.

He explained how the harness was worn. How the rod was located in the massive socket on the stern of the boat. How the fliers of line went out at right angles to the launch to very long rods pointing to the sky at ·45 degrees, resting at the tip of each before streaming back in the sea which ran to the horizon. We were out from the shore some thirty miles.

We cruised and asked innumerable questions of our ghillie/captain. What signs are we looking for? What is that sole porpoise doing on its own over there? The sea was quite rough with a long deep swell prohibiting a full view of the surface half the time. And could we expect a marlin – blue, black or striped; or a wahoo or big shark? We looked quite professional.

It was a long time of coming, then suddenly a

scream. The line fled off the tip of the outrigger and we had become deepsea fishermen.

Wonderful noise – music – lovely.

The ghillie got the boat about and put on power. We were in contact with a great deep sea fish. The line kept whizzing off the reel. Our expedition had come to fruition.

Suddenly the singing reel was silent.

All the line had gone with our deep sea monster – so no fish!

Shattered undergraduate team. Rather cross ghillie.

And who was to pay for the line?

Sunbathing was resumed.

We had to content ourselves being photographed beside the splendid catches of immense sail fish and marlin caught by real fishers, as they hung on the quay side.

It lingers in the memory.

Hank did try

"A SHARK!" "A SHARK!"

NOTHING daunted, some years later I found myself making the greetings speech for my profession at the Annual Meeting of our American colleagues in Miami. My wife and I had a brief holiday thereafter down the Florida Keys.

It was a very basic hut we hired, just one room. The windows were covered with netting, not glass and a solid door hinged along the top in front of each of them, which had to be propped open for ventilation.

When it rained we had to be sure that the windows on the windward side were closed. Awkward in the middle of the night when the wind changed direction. Out we had to go in the rain and let down the windward window/doors to keep the rain out. The lee ones had to be opened. They were of course wet having had the rain. Something had to be kept open because the humidity was oppressive.

Otherwise it was quite comfortable.

Deep sea fishing is rather expensive, but 'a-fishing we would go'.

The boat was not much larger than those to be seen on the lakes in Hyde Park and Regent's Park. And the pair of us plus our ghillie put us pretty low in the water. I was rather nervous of what would happen if we got into a really big fish.

Early in the day, ghillie Buzzy Bushnell met us and took us to a pier (just an oversized wooden jetty) and there we could see lots of small fish swimming around in the sea. These were to be our live bait, so we fished for a while (sometimes netting them) to fill Buzzy's bait container. Then out we set for the Straits of Florida or the Gulf of Mexico.

My knowledge of deep sea fishing was minimal, secret and alarming. My previous expedition off Florida sensed that a big fish was possible. So what do we do then with a small boat like this with not a great deal of power to turn on, when a hooked fish starts moving?

And my wife caught a shark.

It was 2½ pounds.

"Can't have been long since it left its mother," we all agreed. Buzzy was pleased that the two foreigners had taken a fish and were excited about their catch. I was relieved that it was a small fish and delighted that it was my wife who caught it. Buzzy showed much enthusiasm about filleting the shark when we went ashore. A happy surgical feat.

That evening we had a splendid meal. The filleted fish was cooked in our one room and served with Lima beans and a lemon sauce. My wife dressed the dish with splendour. The flesh was like chicken with the taste of fish.

Incidentally, when we opened our bags back in New York the contents were soaking wet – the humidity of the Florida Keys.

YES, IT CAN GO TO YOUR HEAD

BACK in the Highlands in Scotland on one occasion, it was so wet and cold we had to eat our lunch standing up under some trees. The rain went off a bit. There was a long narrow off-shoot from the loch nearby, the Canal as it is called. The banks were low and there were no trees. The wind was helpful, nearly behind me.

With my first cast I had a trout. I took two more out of the same pool twenty minutes later. They were just under the half-pound each. What splendid natural flies were on that water, cinnamon and gold and jet black ones as well. I had six 'take-home' trout. Success and fresh air were heady stuff.

When I got back to the hotel I saw a very large fish lying on the wall right beside the front door. I didn't know what kind of fish it was and fortunately just before I said 'Salmon' someone said 'Pike'. But I wasn't saved from my second mistake. "About four pounds?" The owner piped up: "Thirteen pounds!"

So, I retreated in silence to learn not to guess the weight of other folk's fish.

There are other signs of the effect the dynamic atmosphere of a highland stream can have on the mind suggesting it has gone to the head.

We took a young Canadian to fish with us at Invermoriston. (Incidentally, we had not been at the Hotel ten minutes when a local gamekeeper reversed his Landrover into our ancient Bentley.)

Dave took one look down the long gentle sloping hillside to the river and charged down, rod in hand, Rodeo fashion, whooping and shouting with delight.

So, what did the trout do?

Rodeo fashion

YOUR VERY OWN WATER

MEDICAL pathology laboratories and trout may sound like the parallel of 'work' and 'play', but if 'trouting' gets into your system you may find yourself using one to help with the other.

Trout watching at home can be achieved. We may not produce the whole effect of the river or the mountain loch in our back garden, but each expedition with a ghillie feeds that searching part of the mind and the hope of having nature nearby in the late evenings or early mornings when the telephone is less likely to ring.

There are many ways of doing this, even in the unpromising areas of Britain where the geography does not supply high hills and wild running water. Suffolk is one such area. What is 'a trout man' to do?

Living in the heart of extensive and intensive farm land there are experienced countrymen available. Bert Cracknell was our man. He was Head Cowman to the 3,000 acre estate beside our cottage. The care of animals was in his blood. Wild flowers, difficult weeds, the best grasses, pond life he knew. And Bert took on our fish.

A large farm would be sure to have in its yard a horse pond for cooling and washing down these famous Suffolk Punch horses which used to pull the plough. To supply the extra water needed for today's cereal growing, some large horse ponds were bulldozed out to a depth of fourteen feet.

My wife and I had the opportunity of taking on just such a pond belonging to farming friends, to design and plant up its new high banks and to decide how many trout it could hold. At our cottage a few miles away we turned all that experience to good use.

Landscaping became an intensive activity. We marked out a piece of land next to the house (we had ten acres which we farmed) and got in the bull-dozers. We reduced by eight feet, the height of the field over an area of one hundred yards by eighty. This of course included the area of the high bank of the existing pond, which we were able to double in size and depth. We left an island in the middle and planted lots of reeds, bulrushes, irises for nesting wild ducks.

There are conditions which have to be met for the growth of trout; chemically correct fresh water, oxygenating weeds, bushes on the bank for the hatch of fly.

A sample of the water was taken to the Harley Street medical pathology laboratory for analysis. Weighted wire baskets with oxygen producing weed were placed all around on the base of the new pond. Heavy slabs of slate on stones were located on the gravel area where a small spring existed. This was to protect the surface and give the trout hiding places against future attack by the heron. The island had more trees planted on it.

So, now for some trout.

In Harley Street we lived 'over the shop', so, off to Billingsgate fish market very early in the morning, say five thirty a.m. A porter there takes a plastic bag, big as a large coal bag, and he places at least two more inside that one to toughen this 'carrier'. In go six buckets of water and then some nice trout. The bag is now collapsed over the water and held closed. A pipe is passed through the collapsed entrance and oxygen is pumped in to fill the bag, it is then properly sealed.

Back to the practice, the bath is half filled with water. The bag of water, trout and oxygen, UNOPENED, is allowed to sit in the cool bath all day. And so to Suffolk in the evening for release. The system worked, and the trout grew and prospered.

On one occasion we were having some replacement trout from a hatchery in Lincolnshire. Half way home I looked into the boot of the car and discovered that one bag had considerably less oxygen than when we started. So, we whizzed into a chemist's shop in a small town in Norfolk and requested, to the astonishment of the pharmacist, some oxygen for our trout.

The oxygenating weed was a great success (my wife has green fingers). The trout, at first fed with special granules, soon got the larvae, nymphs, flies, weed, snails, which was home to them. They needed no further artificial food.

Our guests thought we were joking when we suggested they might like to see our trout. A handful of bread crumbs and we had a circus in the water any time.

Water Keeper Bert advised on the overgrowth of grass and weed and kept an eye on icing of the pond in winter. But when the whole pond froze suddenly, a fox got to the island and our ducks . . .

We also invented a system for keeping the water level high at times of drought by connecting a levelling gauge in the pond to an electric pump at the bottom of our cottage well. There was an endless supply of fresh water from 120 feet down, so the water level could be protected all the time.

TWENTY-TWO GHILLIES LATER

WHEN to fish, where to fish, when to sit and talk, are just the beginning of a day out with a ghillie. We sense the depth of his wisdom when he says in his country accent: "It will take more than human wisdom to get us up this hill in the world today."

Ghillies do not have much choice of guests, but they have a remarkable diagnosis of the character of those whom they look after.

Donald Campbell had endless patience. His "Oh's" had to be paid attention to, and I was not too understanding those early days. He gave all round care: "The fish are dour"; "Some fine fish come out of this place"; "Don't do too much or ye'll tire your arm."

The unspoken challenge was that I was being introduced to the world outside the tight channels of a successful professional life. He sensed the stress in me and began to raise, without labelling it, the consideration we must give to our motives. Looking back, he was saying: "What are you in it for?" That question has great depth.

Robbie Ross understood the vast features of the countryside, with thunderstorm and equally compelling quietness of the glen. We did a marathon over the mountains, with our rod. He made the variety of impressions which feed the mind as clinical research does.

John Macaskill had all the verve of a Lovat Scout and showed the varieties of skills to match the commitment of any professional.

John McIntyre, in his gentle manner, gave

the disciplines needed and the bond of friendship of the river bank.

Seumas almost said I needed to move beyond my specialist professional attitudes, showing already in my fishing. He opened my mind to the width of techniques which attract millions to angling.

Jim Haddrell produced a flood barrier to the enthusiasms of the ill-taught fisherman and might have said: "The knock-about act stops here." This approach appeals to the man who has an eye to the future.

The committed research worker sees the depth of understanding inbuilt in the ghillie: patience; perspective; skills; disciplines; knowledge; minutiae of detail; challenge. And an over-riding dimension not got by human application.

My conviction is that the maturity of a real countryman, the ghillie, is in line with the solid structure, basic requirement, of Western thinking.

We live in a puff of time. We are lucky to have behind us a strand of sound thinking coming up all the way from Socrates (399 B.C.). He had the art of sorting out "Wind Eggs" from "Core Truths". We could do with some of that today.

It is a myth to think that Information Technology will deal with our pressures. All it does is speed up the processes.

We rush about in Economics. We may even go back to Scotsman Adam Smith. But few today have any idea who he was, unless they move deeper than the confusions of modern economists, who fail to study the real balance Smith presented. His important work was *not* his *Wealth of Nations*, but his *Theory of Moral Sentiments*. Smith was defining what is needed to be the kind of people fitted to deal with a massive change in world affairs. This is surely relevant today.

How to survive the coming flood of information and disinformation? Soon we will not be able to cope mentally without a special filter for the forefront of the mind. This filter is a built-in feature of the ghillie. It is there because of his understanding of nature.

Lifting the curtain on another part of the mind in conversation with ghillies, suggests that we re-examine the basis of our excellence back home, a basic requirement in considering the stress of life. But how to do it, if one's targets are 'skill and cash'? This calls for a radical change in our nature, nothing less. Therein lies the answer to stress.

My observations of many of them cause me to liken them to Socrates, because the more I got to know them, the more I found them to be midwives of the mind.

The wise man will make the time to stand back from his accustomed targets. He will make the time to find ways of having a satellite view of the streams of world thinking and what is behind them. He will accept that his excellence is normal, just like breathing. It just makes him fit to move on a road of discovery.

These ghillies encouraged me in my investigation into the human nature behind stress. Resolution is available to anyone. The intellect alone, however brilliant, will not produce the new thinking needed today.

Behind the wisdom of my ghillies has been the inference that a supreme being has a plan for every life. When this is accepted, strain and breakdown become a thing of the past. A great filtering process takes place in the mind.

AFTERTHOUGHT

SUCCESS is the order of the day in bioche-mistry. Breathtaking in its newness is human cell biology engineering. No longer will the human body be flooded with a medicine when we are ill, hoping that some of it might reach that sore toe or that painful tooth which is what we are complaining about. What we will be given will be labelled: *For the sick part only.* And so many side effects will be avoided.

For some 'the Balance of Payments' and "a few minutes ago the Dow Jones Average in New York was . . .", is their order of the day.

So, how to prepare for tomorrow's revolution in ideas? How to prepare for "The boiler house", as Bill McLaren, our super-Scot rugby commentator calls the place where the action takes place in the second row of the scrum?

Observe today's typical media headline: *"The adrenalin is running! The pressure is on!"* These jargon clips about our sporting heroes will soon be superseded. Medical cell engineering is uncovering the molecule which sets in motion the whole chemical process. The science journal will tell you: " . . . Just put together, 41-amino-acids in the right configuration . . . and you have the stress molecule." Actually, when this has been done, there will still be something missing. There is a difference between knowledge and wisdom.

Today's requirement is not the study of knowledge of scientific judgements, but the study of wisdom and value judgements.

The Press carries a plethora of ideas about enouraging our body defence or exposing the lack of it, against modern viral disease.

The body's physical defence system is called its immune system. It is in-built and has a full range of activity from the minimal requirement, when we have a cut finger in need of healing, right along to the magic of recovery from a winter cold, without any medical help at all. We cured ourselves.

We have to encourage the body's own defences to be sharp and to neutralise invaders. But there is more to the therapy we need than physical defence, and the therapy offered by the ghillie is in this field. It is rarely said, but the therapy available could be expressed as it was more than 2,000 years ago by Plato, that the primary aim of thinking was statesmanship. The development not of power-seeking men, but advisers to those in power and the growth of nations from tyrannical structure to reformed constitutions.

Service is here represented not as a secondary role in life, but the title role. The ghillie's wisdom about nature and his sense of service affecting the human mind is at the core of the ghillie's life. It is as basic as the discovery of the wheel. The invention of the wheel put society into a state of flux by the innovations of its use. Modern technology is doing the same. But the lessons of nature are available to those sensible enough to expose themselves to them.

What the ghillie is offering is the encouragement of growth of a defence system for the mind. A system as practical as the body's physical defence system. An immune system for our thinking and beliefs.

This happens to be the area in greatest need of its research workers, the structure of an immune system for decision-making.

That is why these men are essential.